MEMOIRS AND SERVICES OF THE
EIGHTY-THIRD REGIMENT

MEMOIRS AND SERVICES
OF THE
EIGHTY-THIRD REGIMENT
COUNTY OF DUBLIN

FROM 1793 TO 1907

INCLUDING

THE CAMPAIGNS OF THE REGIMENT
IN THE WEST INDIES, AFRICA, THE PENINSULA, CEYLON, CANADA, AND INDIA

LONDON
HUGH REES, Ltd.
119, PALL MALL, S.W.
1908

ALL RIGHTS RESERVED

THE EIGHTY-THIRD REGIMENT

"CAPE OF GOOD HOPE"

"TALAVERA."   "BUSACO."   "FUENTES D'ONOR"

"CIUDAD RODRIGO"

"BADAJOS."   "SALAMANCA."   "VITTORIA"

"NIVELLE"

"ORTHES."   "TOULOUSE."   "PENINSULA"

"CENTRAL INDIA"

PREFACE

This Memoir of the Services of the 83rd (County of Dublin) Regiment, now 1st Battalion Royal Irish Rifles, was originally arranged and prepared for publication, from September, 1793, "in which year the Regiment was raised," to September, 1863, by Brevet Major Edward William Bray, who was then serving with the Regiment. The later history, from 1864 up to present time, has been collected from the Authentic Records preserved in the Regimental Orderly Room.

MEERUT,
    December, 1907.

CONTENTS

PART I contains the Services of 1st Battalion, from 1793, the date of its being raised, to 1817, when the 1st and 2nd Battalions were amalgamated at the Cape of Good Hope.

PART II contains the History of the 2nd Battalion from 1804 to 1814, and the Services of the Regiment during the Peninsular War.

PART III contains the Services of the Regiment in Ceylon from 1814 to 1829.

PART IV contains the Services of the Regiment from 1829 to 1848, including its Services in Canada.

PART V contains the Services of the Regiment in India, including the Indian Mutiny, from 1849 to 1857.

PART VI contains the Services of the Regiment from 1858 to 1863, including the campaign of 1858 in Central India.

PART VII contains the Services of the Regiment from 1864 to 1907, including the campaign of 1881 in South Africa.

MEMOIRS

OF THE

EIGHTY-THIRD REGIMENT

PART I

SERVICES OF THE 1st BATTALION, 1793-1817

1793. IN September, 1793, Major William Fitch obtained a letter of service to raise a regiment, which, after being numbered, became the 83rd, its formation bearing date 28th September, 1793, and of which the major was appointed lieutenant-colonel commandant. The regiment was embodied at Dublin, and quartered in the old Custom House at Essex Bridge for about two months, when it was called upon to take a portion of the garrison duties, in consequence of a great number of troops having been drawn from that garrison for the purpose of embarking for the West Indies. The regiment then moved to the royal barracks. The establishment of the regiment at this period was fixed at 72 sergeants, 26 drummers, 1200 rank and file, and an additional lieutenant added to each company.

1794. In October, 1794, a second battalion was added to the regiment, and the establishment of the first battalion was reduced to 52 sergeants, 22 drummers, and 1000 rank and file. The 2nd Battalion soon afterwards was numbered, and became the 134th Regiment.

On the 7th November, 1794, the regiment embarked at Dublin and sailed for England. It landed at Pill and marched to Bath, in Somersetshire, where it was quartered several months. It then marched to Poole, in Dorsetshire, where it remained about five months, and from thence to Southampton.

1795. On the 5th May, 1795, the regiment embarked at Stokes Bay for the West Indies, and sailed in about ten days afterwards.[1]

On the arrival of the regiment at Martinique, it received orders to proceed to Jamaica, and, after a few days' sail, arrived at Port Royal on the 16th July, 1795.

The regiment was then removed from the chartered ships to men-of-war and transports, and sailed for Saint Domingo; but the Maroon insurrection having broken out a few days after the regiment had sailed, Lord Balcarras, the Governor, despatched a schooner to recall them; but she could only overtake two ships, which returned with about half the regiment, which landed at Mondego Bay and was marched into the interior.

The regiment was actively employed in the suppression of the Maroon insurrection for about eight months, and sustained a loss of 70 killed and wounded; amongst the former was the Lieutenant-Colonel Commandant, William Fitch; and Captains Lee and Brunt slightly wounded—the former died in four days afterwards.

On the 13th September, 1795, Major-General James Balfour succeeded to the colonelcy, vice Lieutenant-Colonel Fitch, killed in action.

---

[1] On clearing the harbour, one of the transports with a company on board was so much damaged by another vessel running foul of her as to be unable to proceed, which company was relanded on the Isle of Wight, and rejoined the head-quarters at Saint Domingo in 1798.

MEMOIRS OF THE 83RD REGIMENT

1798. The few men that remained of the detachment that went to Saint Domingo in 1795 returned to Jamaica in 1798.

1802. The regiment remained on the north side of Jamaica until the beginning of June, 1802, when it embarked in men-of-war at Savannah le Mar, Falmouth, and Mondego Bay, for Port Royal, and on its arrival marched to Spanish Town; shortly afterwards the men were allowed to extend their services in the 60th and 85th, and a few to the 2nd West India Regiment.

On the 4th July, 1802, the regiment embarked on board His Majesty's ship *Delft*, and landed at Portsmouth on the 22nd August following, its strength being 1 lieutenant-colonel, 2 majors, 9 captains, 16 subalterns, 29 sergeants, 11 drummers, and 294 rank and file.

During the service of seven years of the regiment in the West Indies, it received drafts and volunteers from several regiments, amounting to 410 rank and file, and deducting men who were drafted and volunteered on its embarkation from England, the regiment appears to have lost by deaths 870 non-commissioned officers and rank and file, from the period of its arrival in the West Indies to its return to England in August, 1802.

During this period the officers named in the margin also died.[1]

---

[1] Dr. Weir, 6th August, 1795.
Col. Fitch, 12th September, 1795.
Lt. Rawes, 2nd September, 1795.
Capt. Lee, 18th September, 1795.
Ens. Horridge, 24th October, 1795.
Lt. Armstrong, 27th October, 1795.
Lt. Morton, 28th October, 1795.
Lt. Cove, 30th October, 1795.
Capt. Hansald, 9th November, 1795.
Capt. Hay, 14th November, 1795.
Lt. Wilton, 14th November, 1795.
S. Mat. Clancy, 14th November, 1795.
Ens. Byrne, 17th August, 1796.
Ens. Morris, 20th August, 1796.
Capt. Stone, 20th August, 1796.
Lt. Trumane, 20th April, 1797.
Ens. Lawton.
Lt. Batt, 20th August, 1800.
F. Smith, 8th August, 1800.
Ens. Hill, 30th September, 1800.
Major White, 27th November, 1800.
Lt. Gibson, 4th October, 1800.
Capt. Wilson, 7th June, 1801.
Lt. Williams, 1st December, 1800.
Lt. Wright, 12th December, 1801.
Lt. Farrell, 26th January, 1802.

The regiment on disembarking proceeded to Hilsea Barracks, where it remained about three weeks, from whence it proceeded to Chelmsford; and in March, 1803, received the route for Portsmouth, and on its arrival embarked for Jersey, on board the *Acastra* frigate and other vessels; and on its disembarkation was quartered at Grove Hill.

On the 4th May, 1805, the regiment embarked at St. Heliers. It joined the expedition at the Cove of Cork, destined against the Cape of Good Hope, under the command of Lieutenant-General Sir David Baird, and landed at the Cape on the 6th January, 1806; and was actually employed in the reduction of

1806.

that settlement, where its head-quarters were stationed, and where it remained quartered until October, 1817, when it was joined by a large detachment of the 2nd Battalion, under Lieutenant-Colonel Collier, on the reduction of the 2nd Battalion at Armagh in 1817. The whole of the regiment, now reunited, and forming but one battalion henceforward, was collected together at Simon's Bay, Cape of Good Hope, in September, 1817, and embarked for Ceylon on 1st October, 1817.[1]

[1] *Vide* Memoir of 2nd Battalion, commencing in the year 1817.

PART II

HISTORY OF THE 2ND BATTALION, 1804-14, AND SERVICES OF THE REGIMENT DURING THE PENINSULAR WAR

THE 2nd Battalion, 83rd Regiment, was raised in the year 1804; the establishment being fixed at 600 rank and file, under the command of Lieutenant-Colonel Hutchison, who had previously belonged to the 1st Battalion.

The head-quarters of the 2nd Battalion were first established at Horsham Barracks, Sussex, where it remained a few months and was then removed to Chichester, at which place it received a draft of 300 men, chiefly from the 3rd Royal Lancashire Militia.

1805. During the stay of the battalion at Chichester, Lieutenant-Colonel Hutchison was removed to the Staff, and Lieutenant-Colonel Gordon succeeded to the command of the regiment.

1806. The battalion removed to Newport, in the Isle of Wight, whence it sent 270 rank and file, with a proportion of officers and non-commissioned officers (being the entire of the effectives fit for active service), to join the 1st Battalion at the Cape of Good Hope.

In August the battalion marched to Chipping Norton, in Oxfordshire, and in November following removed to Battle Barracks, Sussex, where its establishment was increased to 800 rank and file. After a short stay at this station, it was ordered to Brabourne Leas and Ashford, in Kent, and in March, 1807, proceeded to Portsmouth and embarked for Guernsey.

1807. Having remained a few days there, it re-embarked and sailed for Jersey; and was quartered at St. Owens, in that island.

In September following it embarked for Ireland; but owing to contrary winds, the whole battalion was not assembled at Cove till January, 1808, when it marched to Kinsale, County Cork.

1808. The same month the battalion was marched to Birr, in King's County, where its establishment was augmented to 1000 rank and file, and an additional lieutenant appointed to each company; from this place 14 officers and 214 rank and file were sent to reinforce the 1st Battalion at the Cape of Good Hope.

In the month of May following the battalion marched to Dublin and occupied the Palatine Barracks, and in December marched to Fermoy.

1809. In January, 1809, the battalion marched from Fermoy to Cork, and embarked at Cove for Corunna; but intelligence having been received of the battle of Corunna and the evacuation of Spain by the British, a ship of war was despatched to recall the transports, when the regiment disembarked and marched back to its old quarters at Fermoy.

In March following the battalion received orders to march to Cove, for embarkation for Lisbon, and having been previously inspected by Brigadier-General Rowland Hill, proceeded to Cove, and embarking on board the transports, sailed to join the British army in Portugal.

On the 6th April, 1809, the battalion, 900 strong, under the command of Lieutenant-Colonel Gordon, landed at Lisbon, and was immediately despatched to join the British army, then under the command of Sir John Cradock, at Coimbra. It was there brigaded with the 9th Regiment (1st Battalion), and placed under the command of Brigadier-General Alan Cameron.

CAMPAIGN OF THE DOURO

1809. General Sir Arthur Wellesley, having superseded Sir John Cradock in the command of the army, advanced to the relief of Oporto, then occupied by the French. General Cameron's brigade was placed in General Sherbrook's division, and was actively engaged at the passage of the Douro and the attack on the French in Oporto.

On the 12th May, at the passage of the Douro, Captain Summerfield and the Light Company of the 83rd were amongst the foremost that crossed in the boats, and occupied the Seminary, and Captain Summerfield rendered himself conspicuous by his gallantry n climbing up and endeavouring to secure the iron gate of the building. The remainder of the regiment crossed at Villa Nova, and, having fought their way through the streets of Oporto, came upon the rear of the enemy as, with their artillery, they were moving out of the town.

At this moment the French were exposed to a flank fire from the troops which had occupied the Seminary, the 83rd and 9th at the same time pouring a volley into their rear. The greater part were killed and wounded, and the remainder dispersing, left their guns in possession of the victorious British.

In this affair the battalion had 14 men wounded.

The 2nd Battalion, 83rd, was one of the regiments employed in the pursuit of the French army to the frontiers of Spain; and on the 16th, a little after dark, after a harassing and stormy march, overtook the French rear-guard at Salamonde. The 9th and 83rd immediately attacked, and the French, the greater part of whom were cooking, and quite unprepared, were speedily driven from the position.

The battalion in this affair had 5 men wounded. The pursuit was continued on the 18th to Montalagne; but the whole army subsequently retiring to Abrantes, the 9th and 83rd went into quarters at Tancos, on the banks of the Tagus, about eight leagues from the former place. Here sickness prevailed to such an extent in the whole army, and especially in the 9th regiment, that that corps was obliged to be sent to Lisbon, and its place in General Cameron's brigade was taken by the 61st Regiment, at Oropesa, on the subsequent advance of the army to Talavera.

CAMPAIGN AND BATTLE OF TALAVERA

1809. In all the movements and privations of the British army in this advance the 83rd bore its full share; and on the 27th and 28th July, when under Sir Arthur Wellesley, it fought and won the glorious battle of Talavera. The battalion was most severely engaged, and particularly distinguished itself in the gallant and impetuous charge on the enemy's line, made by General Sherbrook's division with the bayonet.

In this battle, General Alan Cameron's brigade, composed of the 61st and 83rd Regiments, was posted in the left centre of the front line, with the brigade of Guards on its right, and the German Legion on its left, and about 100 paces in its front, occupied by its Light Infantry, was the dry, rocky bed of a mountain torrent. On the 27th, the French attempted to turn the allies' left, and to take a height in front of General Hill's division. In this they were unsuccessful, but the following day, at about 2 p.m., they renewed their efforts, and made a general attack on the whole line.

The battle then recommenced, and raged with redoubled fury. The French guns played with murderous precision on General Cameron's brigade, and the men of the 61st and 83rd Regiments were mowed down by sections.

Under cover of this fire, the French Infantry, in imposing masses, advanced rapidly and steadily to the attack.

The 83rd Regiment had been previously ordered to lie down to avoid the tremendous cannonade directed against it; but on the French battalions nearing the ravine on its front, it rose up, and with the 61st advancing steadily to meet them, allowed their dark columns to approach to within thirty paces of their ranks, then, pouring in a well-directed and destructive volley, it dashed impetuously forward through the ravine, and, charging vigorously with the bayonet, drove the enemy with great slaughter headlong before them.

The regiment followed in pursuit, until it received the command to retire, when, facing about and carrying off its wounded, it steadily recrossed the ravine, and, amid the warm encomiums of General Cameron himself, resumed its original position in the line; this (together with the 61st) it maintained with unflinching resolution till the close of the day, when the French (who had been temporarily successful on the right and left of the brigade) were compelled to return, leaving the victory to the British.

The very severe loss of the 83rd in this hard-fought battle, amounting to nearly half its number present, fully testifies the honourable service it performed.

Its commanding officer, Colonel Gordon, while cheering and leading on his men, fell in the first burst of the glorious charge at their head.

Three lieutenants—Montgomery, Dahman, and Flood—with 2 sergeants and 64 rank and file, were killed with him. Two captains—Summerfield and Reynolds; 7 lieutenants—Abel, Johnstone, Nicholson, Pine, Boggie, Baldwin, and Ferris; 4 ensigns—Lord Tulloch, Barry, Carey, and Irwin; and Adjutant Brahan, with 15 sergeants, 2 drummers, and 265 rank and file, were wounded; making the total casualties of the battalion 365 rank and file killed and wounded, and amongst the latter many were so badly injured that on the subsequent abandonment of Talavera by the Spaniards, the greater part, being unable to move, fell into the hands of the French.

For the services of the regiment in this arduous battle, Sir William Gordon, the brother of Colonel Gordon, received the medal which would have decorated that gallant soldier's breast, had he happily survived the action.

Lieutenant Pine, the subaltern of the Grenadier Company of the 83rd, was promoted to a company in the 66th Regiment for his distinguished valour in hastening to the assistance of the colours—in carrying which through this battle, officer after officer had been shot down. Lieutenant Pine seized one of the colours and bore it gallantly forward, and did not relinquish it till he was himself severely wounded and obliged to be relieved of his honourable burden. Many sergeants also were killed and wounded in protecting the colours through this fierce battle.

Its casualties, however, had so weakened the 83rd, that it was deemed unable to keep the field any longer; it was on this account ordered to Lisbon, and on its departure from the army General Cameron expressed his approbation of the corps, and his appreciation of its conduct in the battle of Talavera, in the following brigade order :—

"BRIGADE ORDERS

"TALAVERA DE LA REAL, *August* 29*th*, 1809.

"The death of Lieutenant-Colonel Gordon, who so gloriously fell at the head of the 2nd Battalion 83rd Regiment, while charging the enemy on the 28th ult., leaves Brigadier-General Cameron the painful necessity of regretting the loss of a sincere friend and gallant officer, and his regiment that of a brave and worthy commander.

"The conduct of the 83rd Regiment in the arduous contest of Talavera merits the Brigadier-General's warmest thanks, and he hopes that Major Napper will justly appreciate the merits of those few that are left.

"The very weak state of the 83rd renders it necessary to send them to Lisbon. The Brigadier-General requests them to accept of his best acknowledgments for their uniform good conduct whilst under his command, and has, at the same time, to assure them that he shall be proud to have the 83rd again in his brigade, when established in health and numbers.

"By order,
"(Signed) H. BALNEAVIS, Captain,
"Acting Brigade Major."

In addition to the above honourable testimonial to its services in this action, the 83rd has been graciously permitted to have the word "Talavera" inscribed on its colours and appointments, in commemoration of its distinguished gallantry in that battle.

The battalion arrived in Lisbon in October, 1809, and remained there till the beginning of September, 1810, during which period Lieutenant-Colonel Collins joined from the 1st Battalion and assumed the command.

In the beginning of September, 1810, the battalion being re-established in health, and numbering 600 rank and file, marched under the command of Lieutenant-Colonel Collins, to join Lord Wellington, at that time retiring to the frontiers of Portugal. It effected its junction with the army the same month, and was placed in the left brigade of the 3rd Division, commanded by General Picton, and in the celebrated division which acquired in the army the distinguished appellation of the "Fighting Division" the 83rd had the honour of serving throughout the remainder of the Peninsular campaigns.

With it, therefore, and its heroic commander, Sir Thomas Picton, the services of the battalion in this memorable war are henceforth identified, being engaged in every skirmish, battle, and assault which this renowned division fought and won, and in every glorious deed of daring and honour it was ever so nobly performing.

On the 26th and 27th of September the battalion was engaged in the actions on the Sierra de Busaco; but the brunt of the battle falling to the good fortune of the right brigade, its casualties were few, amounting only to 1 lieutenant (Lieutenant Colthurst) and 6 rank and file wounded. For the services of the regiment on this occasion Colonel Collins received a medal, and his Majesty was pleased to sanction the word "Busaco" being borne on its colours and appointments.

Shortly after Lieutenant-Colonel Collins was removed to the command of a brigade in the Portuguese service, and the command of the 83rd devolved upon Major H. W. Carr.

After the decisive and signal repulse of the French at Busaco, the British army continued its retrograde movement until it was halted by its skilful commander in the strongly fortified lines of Torres Vedras, and the regiment remained in position in these celebrated lines till the month of March, 1811, when the French, under Marshal Massena, commenced its retreat.

The British army followed in eager and hot pursuit, and the 3rd Division hanging closely on the rear, the 83rd was in constant and warm engagement with the enemy.

It came up with them at Leyria, Pombal, and Condeixa, and in the skirmishes at those places, and at Fleur-de-Lis, Guarda, and Sabugal, its casualties amounted to 2 sergeants and 52 men killed and wounded.

In May following, the battalion was actively engaged in the actions at Fuentes d'Onor, on the 3rd, 4th, and 5th of that month, and was mentioned in Lord Wellington's despatch of the battle, as being distinguished in the defence of the village of Fuentes d'Onor, and the repulse of the enemy therefrom. Its casualties, however, were fortunately but few, amounting to 1 lieutenant (Ferris) and 6 rank and file killed, and 1 lieutenant (Vereker), 1 sergeant, and 22 rank and file wounded, and his Majesty was pleased to sanction the word "Fuentes d'Onor" being inscribed on the colours and appointments of the 83rd, in commemoration of the distinguished conduct of the battalion in that battle.

The same month the battalion was employed in the first siege of Badajoz, and had 6 rank and file wounded in the trenches.

The siege being raised, the regiment assisted in the blockade of Ciudad Rodrigo, and on the 25th September, when Marshal Marmont advanced to the relief of that fortress, the 83rd, with Colville's brigade, then composed of the 5th (2nd Battalion), 77th, 83rd, and 94th Regiments, greatly distinguished itself. On that occasion immense bodies of French cavalry, supported by artillery and infantry, attacked the 5th and 77th Regiments in their position on a hill, covering the road to Guinaldo; but these two gallant regiments nobly sustained their assault, and repeatedly repulsed the enemy. Their flank, however, being threatened, Lord Wellington gave the order to retire, when, being joined by the remaining regiments of the brigade, the whole, driving back the French horsemen whenever they approached them, fell back steadily, until they reached Guinaldo, where they were halted, and joined the day after by the right brigade, which, stationed at Pastores, had been cut off by the movement. In this gallant affair the 83rd had 1 sergeant and 5 rank and file killed, and 3 sergeants and 16 rank and file wounded.

CIUDAD RODRIGO

1812. In the month of January, 1812, the regiment was employed in the siege and capture of Ciudad Rodrigo; and on the 19th of that month, when that fortress was taken by storm, the Light Company of the 83rd, under the Hon. Captain Powys, led the right attack, and escaladed the outwork in front of the castle. The remainder of the battalion lined the trenches and covered the advance of the storming parties of the 3rd Division in their assault on the great breach. The loss of the regiment in the siege amounted to 4 men killed, and 2 lieutenants (Vereker and Matthews) and 12 men wounded; and the word "Ciudad Rodrigo" has been inscribed by the royal authority on its colours and appointments for its services on this occasion.[1]

BADAJOZ

1812. At Badajoz, in April, the same year, the regiments of the 3rd Division were again called upon to display the burning, irresistible courage of British soldiers, and the capture of that fortress by storm on the 6th April was mainly attributed to the impetuous valour with which they escaladed and took the castle.

---

[1] The regiment, and especially the Light Company, were warmly thanked by General Picton for their conduct.

On this, as on former occasions, the 83rd highly distinguished itself, and its services on the 25th March were most conspicuous.

On the 25th March, fire was first opened on Badajoz, and it was determined to storm the outwork, La Picurina, after nightfall on that day. For this purpose, General Kempt, with 500 men from the 3rd Division, was ordered to carry it by assault. These he divided into three divisions, the centre of which, composed of 100 men from the 83rd, under the Hon. Captain Powys, was held in reserve. The flank divisions rushed impetuously to the attack, but the strength of the work, and the destructive musketry of the French, having rendered their courageous efforts fruitless, Powys and his reserve were also sent headlong against it. Running vehemently forward, the men of the 83rd soon cleared the intervening space, and in spite of a most galling fire escaladed the work, at a salient angle, and mounted the rampart. Here a desperate struggle ensued. Powys, first and foremost of his men, fell dangerously wounded, but Sergeant Hazlust of his regiment, defending him stoutly with his halberd, kept the French at bay, and held his ground till the remainder of the men, clambering up thickly and resolutely, came to his aid, and driving the enemy before them, cleared the ramparts, and enabled the flank divisions to enter also. For this gallant service, Captain Powys received the rank of brevet-major, but did not survive to enjoy the fruits of his bravery. With his dying breath, however, the gallant fellow recommended Sergeant Hazlust to the notice of his superiors, and that valiant soldier, for his conduct on this occasion, was almost immediately promoted to be sergeant-major of the battalion.

On the 6th April, also, the memorable night of the storm of Badajoz, the 83rd most successfully and nobly availed itself of the glorious opportunity of distinction afforded it. The distinguished honour of leading the 3rd Division in the assault on the castle was assigned to it, and, rapidly and resolutely filing over the narrow bridge of the little River Rivillas, the regiment rushed impetuously to the walls, and under a most galling and murderous discharge of shells and combustibles, planted the ladders against them. Four out of the seven ladders were broken and destroyed, but officers and men, mounting the remainder, made the most determined efforts to force themselves in, repeatedly driven back and thrown down, crushed and bruised, from the parapets of the ramparts. The 83rd still persevered, and at length Major Carr, Captain Hext, Lieutenant Broomfield, Adjutant Swinburne, with others, followed closely by their men, effected an entrance at the right angle of the work, and established themselves on the rampart. At about the same time, the remainder of the division scaling the wall at another angle, the French turned and made in full flight for the gate. The officers and men of the 83rd rapidly pursued, and closing the gate, and blocking it with stones, wood, and other materials, secured the castle from recapture by the French, who, crowding from the breaches, and pouring volley after volley through it, endeavoured in vain to retake it. The castle thus being won, the French abandoned the remaining defences, and surrendered the fortress to the British.

The regiment's loss in this siege and assault was necessarily very severe, amounting to one-third of its number engaged. Three officers—Captains Powys, Fry, and Ensign Hackett—with 1 sergeant, and 36 rank and file, were killed; and 6 officers—Lieutenants Broomfield, O'Neill, Bowles, Lane, Vavasour, and Baldwin—and 81 rank and file, wounded. Major Carr received a clasp and the rank of lieutenant-colonel, and Captain

Hext that of brevet major, for their own and their regiment's highly distinguished conduct in this assault, and his Majesty has been pleased to permit the 83rd to bear the word "Badajoz" on its colours and appointments, in commemoration of the important and successful service it there rendered.

CAMPAIGN OF SALAMANCA

1812. The fall of Ciudad Rodrigo and Badajoz having opened the way into Spain, the British army was enabled to commence its march into that country, and the 2nd Battalion 83rd, serving throughout the glorious campaign of 1812, had its full share of danger and honour, in the memorable victory of Salamanca, when the French army, under Marshal Marmont, was signally defeated on the 22nd July, 1812.

On that glorious day, the 3rd Division, commanded by Major-General the Hon. Edward Pakenham (General Picton being absent on account of ill-health) was posted in a wood, behind Aldea Tejada, completely concealed from the enemy, and securing the main road to Ciudad Rodrigo. About 2 p.m., the French, endeavouring to turn the British right and gain the road to Ciudad Rodrigo, extended their left in the direction of that fortress, thereby weakening their centre, and affording Lord Wellington the favourable opportunity he had so long desired of attacking them. He immediately took advantage of it, and assailing in front, with the 4th, 5th, 6th, and 7th Divisions, ordered the 3rd Division to attack the French columns, which were moving down on the Ciudad Rodrigo road, and nobly and gallantly did General Pakenham launch the battalions of the "Fighting Division" against the enemy; forming line by regiments, they rushed impetuously forward, and bearing on with resistless force, carried everything before them.

The 83rd Regiment, with Colville's brigade, was in the full brunt of this decisive and successful attack. At one time charging gallantly forward, it overthrew the enemy whenever he stood to meet it; at another, halting, and wheeling by divisions, to allow the British cavalry to pass through, it re-formed, and followed hotly on, encouraging and cheering the pursuing troopers.

Three thousand prisoners were taken by the division this day, and special mention of its commander and it was made by Lord Wellington in his despatch. Colonel Campbell, also, who commanded Colville's brigade (in the absence of that officer commanding the 4th Division), received his lordship's thanks for its services on the occasion.

The casualties of the battalion in this battle amounted to 13 rank and file killed, and 1 lieutenant (Lieutenant Gascoyne) and 32 rank and file wounded; and it had, moreover, the great misfortune to lose, though not in its own ranks, its gallant lieutenant-colonel (Lieutenant-Colonel Collins), who, commanding a Portuguese brigade, had previously, at the sanguinary battle of Albuera, lost a leg, and now, in this great action again distinguishing himself, received a mortal wound.

Lieutenant-Colonel Carr had one horse, and Adjutant Swinburne two horses, shot under them, and in commemoration of the distinguished services of the battalion of the 83rd in this action, his Majesty has been graciously pleased to sanction the word "Salamanca" being inscribed on its colours and appointments.

The battalion was next employed in the investment of the "Retiro," a fortified building at Madrid; at which two men of the battalion were wounded. It subsequently retired with the 3rd Division, when the whole of the army retreated from before Burgos.

CAMPAIGN OF VITTORIA

1813. The next service which the battalion had the good fortune to be engaged in was the triumphant battle of Vittoria, on the 21st June, 1813, when the 83rd bore a prominent part and highly distinguished itself. On that occasion, Colville's brigade being in front, the 83rd had the honour of leading the 3rd Division in its passage across the River Zadara; and the advance of the brigade against the enemy drew forth the especial approbation of Lord Wellington, who mentioned it in his despatch in the following terms :—

"Major-General the Hon. C. Colville's brigade, of the 3rd Division, was seriously attacked in its advance by a very superior force, which it drove in, supported by General Inglis's brigade of the 7th Division, under Colonel Grant, of the 82nd; these officers and the troops under their command distinguished themselves."

Maxwell, an historian of the great duke's life, also, in his description of this memorable victory, thus vividly recounts the advance of Colville's brigade :—

"The subsequent advance of the allied columns against the enemy's right centre was beautifully executed, as in echelon of regiments it crossed the hallowed ground on which tradition placed the chivalry of England when the Black Prince delivered battle to Henry the Bastard, and by a decisive victory replaced Don Pedro on the throne. As if animated by some glorious impulse, the battalions advanced not to combat, but to conquer; Colville's brigade of the 'Fighting Third' led the attack, and the first enemy's corps that confronted it was gallantly defeated. Pressing on with characteristic impetuosity, and without halting to correct the irregularity a recent and successful struggle had occasioned, the brigade encountered on the brow of the hill two lines of French infantry, regularly drawn up, and prepared to receive the assailants. For a moment the result was regarded with considerable apprehension, and means were adopted by Lord Wellington for sustaining the brigade, when (as that event seemed inevitable) it should be repulsed by the enemy; but valour overcame every disadvantage, and the perfect formation of the French could not withstand the dashing onset of the assailants; their rush was irresistible. On went the daring soldiers, sweeping before them the formidable array which, circumstanced as they were, appeared calculated to produce annihilation."

The 83rd, moreover, had this day the good fortune to obtain particular commendation from General Colville himself; with the 94th it attacked and captured a battery of guns, and in an assault on a village, led by General Colville in person, the men of the 83rd rendered themselves so conspicuous by their daring valour, that he directed Adjutant Swinburne (who, with Lieutenants Hingston, Barry, C. O'Neill, and Volunteer Nugent, were also distinguishing themselves at that particular point) to take the names of a large number of them, to whom, after the action, he awarded a guinea apiece.

The casualties of the 83rd in this glorious victory were severe: 3 officers (Major Widrington, Lieutenants Lindsey and Bloxham), 4 sergeants, and 28 rank and file were killed; and 4 officers (Captain Venables, Lieutenants J. Smith, Baldwin, and Barry), with 6 sergeants and 68 rank and file, were wounded. Its gallant conduct in the battle was acknowledged by medals being awarded to its commanding officer, Colonel Carr, and to Major Hext. Volunteer Nugent also was appointed to an ensigncy in the battalion, and his Majesty was graciously pleased to permit the word "Vittoria" being inscribed on the colours and appointments of the 83rd, in commemoration of the distinguished service it rendered in that battle.

After this crowning victory, Lord Wellington undertook the sieges of San Sebastian and Pampeluna, and the 3rd Division was employed in the investment of the latter place; but being shortly after relieved by the 7th Division, it was formed in right support of the remainder of the army, which was so disposed as to cover the operations against these strong and important fortresses.

On the 25th and 26th of July, the French under Marshal Soult having, after a desperate struggle, forced the Roncesvalles and Maya Passes, General Picton moved his division up in support, and, forming in order of battle on the right of the 4th Division, in front of Huarte, and extending to the hills beyond Olaz, there awaited the further advance of the French.

In the ensuing hard-fought battles on the 27th and 28th July, the brunt of the fight fell to the good fortune of the 4th Division, and the 3rd was but slightly engaged. Its picquets and light infantry, however, skirmished with the enemy's tirailleurs, and the division itself advancing on the right of the victorious 4th, turned the enemy's left and completed his signal repulse. In this affair the battalion lost only 8 men wounded.

The French having been thus driven back, the siege of San Sebastian was prosecuted with redoubled vigour; and at last, after a second most sanguinary assault, the city was carried by storm. Pampeluna also having been reduced, the British general led his victorious troops from their lofty positions, and, descending from the snow-clad summits of the Pyrenees, launched them on the fair and fertile provinces of France.

On the 10th of November, 1813, 90,000 men descended to the fight, and, rushing simultaneously from various points on the entrenched and strongly fortified lines of the enemy, commenced the battle of Nivelle; and here again the "Fighting Third Division" signally availed itself of the glorious opportunity for distinction afforded it. Led by General Charles Colville (in the absence of Picton in England), the division attacked the left centre of the enemy's position, and carrying everything before it, won the bridge of Amotz, and seizing the heights between that structure and the fortified redoubt called Louis XIV, established itself firmly on them. It then attacked the enemy in flank, while he was assailed in front by the 4th and 7th Divisions, stormed the redoubt, hurled the enemy headlong out of it, and, afterwards crossing the Nivelle, attacked him on the heights on that side of the river also, and gained triumphant and secure possession of them.

In this battle, as on former occasions, the 83rd was in the heat of the engagement, and proved itself worthy of the noble division to which it belonged.

Its casualties amounted to 10 rank and file killed, and 5 officers (Lieutenants Watson, Barry, and Wyatt, Ensigns Burgess and ———[1]), and 28 rank and file wounded; and the royal authority has been received for the regiment to bear the word "Nivelle" on its colours and appointments, to commemorate its gallantry in that action.

The next service the regiment was employed in was the passage of the Gare d'Oleron, when the 3rd Division, under General Picton himself, attacked the ford above the bridge at Sauvetterre; the regiment, with the left brigade commanded by Colonel Keane, was in this encounter warmly engaged, and sustained a loss of

---

[1] Name not in records.

5 rank and file killed, and 12 rank and file wounded, and lost some prisoners from the Light Infantry, which had crossed the river.

At Orthes, on the 27th February, 1814, the 3rd Division was again in the very heat and brunt of battle, and highly distinguished itself, attacking the heights, on which the left and centre of the enemy were strongly posted. It, after severe fighting, gained possession of them, and with the simultaneous assaults of the 52nd Regiment on the left, dislodged the enemy from his position and secured the victory.

The loss of the 83rd in this action was severe, amounting to 1 sergeant, 10 rank and file killed, 9 officers (Lieutenant-Colonel Carr, Major Blaquiere, Captains Venables and Elliott, Lieutenants Baldwin, Watson, and Lane, Ensign Nugent and Adjutant Swinburne), with 1 sergeant, 1 drummer, and 28 rank and file wounded; and its conduct was so meritorious that Colonel Keane, in brigade orders, returned it and the 87th his thanks for their gallant behaviour, declaring that in this battle they had added to their already high reputation. On this occasion Captain Elliott, of the Light Company, was promoted to be brevet major, and received a medal, and his Majesty was graciously pleased to permit the word "Orthes" to be inscribed on the colours and appointments of the 83rd, to commemorate the service it performed in that battle.

In the month of March following, Picton's division again encountered the enemy, and falling upon him at Vic Bigorre, drove him from his position, and compelled him to continue his retreat.

In this affair the 83rd Regiment was vigorously engaged, and lost 1 sergeant and 6 men killed, and 2 Lieutenants (Hingstone and Lane) and 16 men wounded.

TOULOUSE

1814. On the 10th April, the British army fought and won the crowning battle of Toulouse, and Picton again led his division into the middle of the fight. The 83rd Regiment, with the left brigade, was but partially engaged and suffered a slight loss, and it has received the royal commission to bear the word "Toulouse" on its colours and appointments, for its services in that victory.

The war was at this period brought to a conclusion; the illustrious Emperor of the French, Napoleon Bonaparte, being compelled to abdicate. His able lieutenant, Marshal Soult, gave in his adhesion to the new government, and hostilities accordingly ceased.

The 83rd was quartered at La Mao, where Major Blaquiere, having recovered from his wounds, rejoined and assumed the command. It was afterwards removed to Blanque Fort Camp, near Bordeaux, where 1 captain, 2 lieutenants, 1 assistant-surgeon, and 15 rank and file joined from prisoners of war.

The whole army was there reviewed by the Duke of Wellington; and on the 1st of June the battalion embarked from Bordeaux for England.

As a reward for their own and their regiment's service during this memorable war, his Majesty was pleased to appoint Lieutenant-Colonel H. W. Carr a Knight Commander, and Major George Hext a Companion, of the Most Honourable Military Order of the Bath; and the word "Peninsula," inscribed by the royal authority on the colours and appointments of the 83rd, commemorates the valiant achievements of the 2nd Battalion throughout the whole of the Peninsular campaigns.

PART III

SERVICES OF THE REGIMENT IN CEYLON FROM 1814-29

1814. ON the 4th July, 1814, the 2nd Battalion embarked on board transports for Ireland, and on the 24th following disembarked at Monkstown, County Cork, and marched into the Fort of Kinsale.

On the 10th of September the battalion marched to Clonmel, and on the 30th of October to Kilkenny, when most of the companies were detached to do duty in the adjacent villages.

On the 9th of November the depôt joined from Maldon in Essex, consisting of 1 major, 7 lieutenants, 5 ensigns, 10 sergeants, 4 drummers, and 192 rank and file, under Major Sullivan, who assumed the command of the battalion.

1815. On the 26th January, 1815, the regiment marched for Dublin, from which place all the officers belonging to the 1st Battalion then doing duty with the 2nd were ordered to join it at the Cape of Good Hope.

1816. In the month of March, 1816, the battalion marched for Armagh, and was detached in that and the neighbouring counties.

At this place Lieutenant-Colonel Cother, C.B., from the half-pay of the 71st, assumed the command.

1817. The 2nd Battalion was inspected by Major-General Barnet on the 24th April, 1817, and disbanded the same day, having previously selected all the serviceable non-commissioned officers and men (consisting of 8 sergeants, 4 drummers, and 381 rank and file), to be held in readiness to join the 1st Battalion, supposed to be in the island of Ceylon, for which station it had been a considerable time under orders.

The major-general expressed his perfect approbation of the battalion during its stay in Armagh, in a district order, wishing the officers every success in future.

There were 15 sergeants, 7 drummers, and 164 rank and file (chiefly wounded men) discharged in consequence of the reduction of the 2nd Battalion.

The route for the march of the detachment was received on the 22nd May, 1817, for Fermoy in two divisions, where it arrived on the 11th and 12th of June. The detachment and depôt received a further route for Cork on the 26th June, from whence the former proceeded in steamboats to Cove, and embarked on board the transports *Adamant* and *Eliza*, under the command of Lieutenant-Colonel Cother, C.B.

The detachment sailed from the Cove on the 7th July, 1817, and arrived in Simon's Bay, Cape of Good Hope, on the 22nd September following, and joined the head-quarters of the regiment, under the command of Lieutenant-Colonel Brunt in Simon's Town.

During the services of the 1st Battalion at the Cape of Good Hope, five companies of the regiment, under the command of Brevet Major Summerfield, were ordered to proceed to the frontier of Africa, in consequence of a revolt of a great number of Boers and Hottentots, joined with the Caffres. This detachment landed at Algoa Bay, and on its disembarkation proceeded to Graaff Reinet, on the banks of Sunday's River, being a march of 350 miles, through a barren country. This revolt having been amicably settled, the detachment returned to Algoa Bay in October,

1816, where it remained until September of the following year.

The head-quarters, etc., embarked, and the regiment sailed from Simon's Bay on the 1st October, and arrived at Colombo, island of Ceylon, on the 16th November and 3rd December, 1817.

1817. The insurrection in the "Kandyan"[1] provinces of Ceylon having commenced a few weeks previous to the arrival of the regiment in that colony, nearly the whole of the battalion, then consisting of 4 field-officers, 10 captains, 32 subalterns, 48 sergeants, 22 drummers, and 969 rank and file, was marched into the interior, and was actively employed in the suppression of the rebellion. During this service the regiment suffered much from climate and privation of every description; the loss in killed and wounded only amounted to 12, but the regiment sustained a loss of 3 officers,[2] 3 sergeants, 3 drummers, and 112 rank and file by disease, and previous to the effects of this campaign being eradicated a further loss of 1 officer,[3] 4 sergeants, and 86 rank and file, making a total of 209 deaths within two years after the landing of the regiment in Ceylon.

1819. On the 9th July, 1819, the regiment, commanded by Lieutenant-Colonel Cother, was inspected by General Sir Robert Brownrigg, Bart., G.C.B., Governor and Commander-in-Chief of the forces in Ceylon, by whom the regiment was very highly complimented.

---

[1] During the Kandyan War, Captain Trydell, in command of the Light Company of the 83rd, attacked a formidable body of rebels posted within the lofty walls of a temple, five miles from Ballengadde, drove them out, and defeated them with considerable loss.

[2] Lieutenant Cautwell, Lieutenant Smith, Ensign Macnae.

[3] Lieutenant Cox.

1820. On the 23rd September, 1819, the following detachment, under the command of Captain Campbell, joined the regiment from the depôt, viz., 89 rank and file, and on the 7th January, 1820, a further detachment of 20 rank and file, under the command of Lieutenant Mee, via New South Wales and Calcutta.

On the 25th December, 1818, the establishment of the regiment was reduced in conformity with the instructions, dated War Office, 23rd November, 1818, to the following numbers, viz., 1 colonel, 1 lieutenant-colonel, 2 majors, 10 captains, 20 subalterns, 5 staff, 35 sergeants, 22 drummers, and 650 rank and file.

1821. On the 12th March, 1821, the regiment[1] was inspected by Major-General Sir Edward Barnes, K.C.B., commanding the forces, who issued a very complimentary order on the occasion.

The 73rd Regiment having received orders in June, 1820, to return to England, the men of that corps were allowed to transfer their services to other regiments in Ceylon, when 140 non-commissioned officers and rank and file volunteered to the 83rd Regiment.

On the 5th September, 1821, the regiment was again inspected by Major-General Sir Edward Barnes, K.C.B., and the regiment, still commanded by Lieutenant-Colonel Cother, was again highly complimented.

1822. On the 25th February, 1822, the regiment was reduced to the following numbers, viz., 1 colonel, 1 lieutenant-colonel, 2 majors, 8 captains, 16 subalterns, 5 staff, 29 sergeants, 12 drummers, and 576 rank and file.

1823. Agreeably to general orders issued by Major-General James Campbell, C.B., the head-quarters of the regiment, consisting of 1 field officer, 4 captains,

[1] Under the command of Lieutenant-Colonel Cother.

3 staff, 12 sergeants, 14 drummers, and 303 rank and file, embarked on the 22nd January, 1823, under the command of Major Summerfield, for Trincomalee, and arrived at that station on the 8th of the following month.

On the 20th March, 1823, Lieutenant-General John Hodgson succeeded to the colonelcy of the regiment vice General James Balfour, deceased.

1824. The head-quarters, etc., of the regiment embarked at Trincomalee, on board several vessels, between the 26th March and 31st October, 1824, and were all landed and collected at Colombo on the 6th November following.

A few months previous to the regiment leaving Trincomalee, the Governor, Lieutenant-General Sir Edward Barnes, received orders for its return to England, but the Burmese War having broken out, the battalion was detained, and ordered to proceed to Kandy, to relieve the 45th Regiment, which corps had been a considerable time under orders for India.

1825. On the 25th September, 1825, the establishment of the regiment was increased to 10 companies, consisting of the following numbers : 6 service companies—2 field officers, 6 captains, 12 subalterns, 5 staff, 30 sergeants, 10 drummers, and 516 rank and file ; 4 depôt companies—1 field officer, 4 captains, 8 subalterns, 1 staff, 12 sergeants, 4 drummers, and 224 rank and file.

The regiment was stationed in Kandy from January, 1825, to October, 1825, when it received the route for Colombo, preparatory to embarkation for England, on board the transports *Amity* and *Arab ;* the former vessel, with the head-quarters division, under Lieutenant-Colonel Cother, .C.B., sailed on the 4th December, and the latter, under Brevet Lieutenant-Colonel Kelly, with the remainder of the regiment, a few days afterwards.

During the services of the regiment in Ceylon (a period of eleven years) it sustained a loss by deaths of 17 officers and 491 non-commissioned officers and rank and file.

Upon the embarkation of the regiment at Colombo, his Excellency Lieutenant-General Sir Edward Barnes, K.C.B., was pleased to issue a most complimentary order to the regiment on its departure from Ceylon for England. Lieutenant-Colonel Cother, the commanding officer, was particularly complimented by the lieutenant-general, and Lieutenant-Colonel Kelly was especially mentioned for his talents and exertions during the Kandyan rebellion.

1829. After a passage of about five months, the regiment arrived in England on the 16th April, and on the 18th May, 1829, landed at Gosport, and was quartered at Forton Barracks, where it remained till the 27th August following; from which place it embarked on board the transports *Hope, Amphitrite,* and *William Harris,* for Scotland, and landed at Leith a few days afterwards and marched to Glasgow.

PART IV

SERVICES OF THE REGIMENT FROM 1829-48

ON the 3rd December, 1829, Major the Hon. Henry Dundas, M.P., succeeded to the lieutenant-colonelcy, vice Cother, who retired.

1830. The regiment was stationed at Glasgow until the 16th August, 1830, when it embarked on board steam-vessels for Belfast, in Ireland, and on landing marched to Enniskillen.

During the stay of the regiment at Enniskillen, it furnished detachments to Omagh, Lifford, Sligo, and Ballyshannon, and on the 1st November, 1831, proceeded to Castlebar.

1832. The regiment was quartered at Castlebar until the 23rd October, 1832, when it received a route for Limerick, at which place the head-quarters arrived on the 29th of the same month.

During the stay of the regiment at Castlebar, it furnished detachments to Drunnore, Westport, Foxford, Ballinrobe, and Tuam.

The cholera having made its appearance in the corps,[1] on the 26th June, 1832, the whole of the men at head-quarters, consisting of 5 companies, and staff, were ordered into camp at Ballinew, about a mile distant from the town, and remained encamped until the 5th of September, when instructions were received to re-occupy the barracks. The regiment lost 10 men by

[1] Died: Assistant-Surgeon G. R. Watson, Lieut. H. S. G. Bowles.

this disease at Castlebar, and 2 officers fell victims to this malady at Ballinrobe.

The regiment removed to Limerick in 1832, when it furnished detachments to Newcastle, Bruff, Galbally, Kilfinnan, Tipperary, and Killaloe.

The officers named in the margin[1] died at this station.

On the 11th August, 1833, the regiment received a route for Dublin, where it arrived on the 19th of that month.

1834. On the 22nd of February, 1834, the regiment received a letter of readiness to proceed to Cork for embarkation to Halifax, Nova Scotia, and on the 5th of April the 1st division embarked on board the *Innisfaile* steamer, and landed at Cork on the next day; the head-quarters division following a few days afterwards.

The separation of the service and depôt companies took place on the 1st April, and the latter, under Major Trydell, proceeded to Mullingar.

During the stay of the regiment at Dublin, the officer named in the margin[2] died.

The service companies, consisting of 2 field officers, 6 captains, 18 subalterns, 5 staff, 30 sergeants, 10 drummers, and 479 rank and file, embarked at Cork, on board the freight ships *Brunswick* and *Rickers*, on the 21st April and 15th May, 1834, and landed at Halifax, Nova Scotia, on the 26th May and 20th June following.

Cholera having made its appearance in the town of Halifax, the three companies at head-quarters were ordered into camp at Windmill Hill, a short distance from the barracks, on the 8th September, and remained encamped until the 1st October. The regiment only lost one man by this disease.

---

[1] Major T. Summerfield, Lieutenant Hon. R. Clifford.
[2] Lieutenant R. Coghlan.

On the 30th September of this year, Major-General Hastings Frazer, C.B., succeeded to the colonelcy of the regiment vice Lieutenant-General Hodgson, removed to the 4th Foot.

The companies which had been stationed at Cape Breton, Prince Edward's Island, etc., since the arrival of the regiment at Halifax, returned to the head-quarters on the 17th, 18th, and 20th July of this year.

1836. During this year the regiment remained stationary at Halifax, Nova Scotia.

1837. The regiment remained in Nova Scotia until the 29th June, 1837, when, in consequence of the unsettled state of Lower Canada, orders were received for its embarkation for Quebec on board her Majesty's frigate *Vestal* and *Champion* sloop of war. The headquarters landed on the 12th, and the remaining companies on the 13th July, occupying the citadel barracks.

During the services of the regiment at Nova Scotia, a period of about three years, it sustained a loss by deaths of 23 rank and file.

Upon the embarkation of the regiment, Major-General Sir Colin Campbell, K.C.B., was pleased to issue a complimentary order, Lieutenant-Colonel Hon. H. Dundas at this time commanding.

On the 3rd August, 1 sergeant and 20 rank and file proceeded to Gross Isle, and returned to the head-quarters on the 19th October. On the 1st November, Major Trydell, with two companies, embarked for Three Rivers, and having remained at that post about ten days, received instructions to proceed to Montreal.

On the 8th December the head-quarters and remaining four companies received orders to embark the following day for Montreal, and landed at that station on the 11th, occupying part of the Quebec Gate barrack.

On the 13th December the regiment formed part

of the brigade under Lieutenant-General Sir J. Colbourne, K.C.B., which proceeded to attack St. Eustache, and were actively engaged in that day's operations.

The following morning the brigade proceeded to Benoit, and returned to Montreal on the 17th December.

1838. In January of this year, two companies proceeded on sleighs to the Upper Provinces, and after remaining some days at St. Thomas, distant about 600 miles from Montreal, one of them, under the command of Lieutenant Kelsall, proceeded to Amherstburg.

The brigands having come over from the American shore and taken possession of Fighting Island, this company, with one of the 32nd, proceeded on the 25th February to disperse them, which service they effectually performed; the brigands leaving behind them a small piece of cannon, with ammunition, muskets, etc. On the 3rd March, this company was again actively employed against the brigands at Peel Island, in conjunction with a part of the 32nd Regiment, and finally rejoined the head-quarters with the other company on the 17th June.

The head-quarters remained at Montreal until the 6th May, when it proceeded viâ the St. Lawrence to Kingston.

On the 11th November, Lieutenant Johnson, with 44 men of the regiment and a party of marines, embarked on board her Majesty's steamboat *Experiment*, with a view to cut off two American schooners, laden with some hundreds of brigands, and whom it was reported they intended to land in the neighbourhood of Prescott. On their arrival, it was discovered that these marauders had effected a landing about a mile and a half below the town, and taken possession of a large stone mill and adjacent houses.

On the morning of the 13th, an attack on the brigands was decided on, and Lieutenant Johnson and a party, with the marines under Lieutenant Parker, reinforced by a number of volunteers, proceeded to attack them. The men advanced under a galling fire from the walls at some distance from the mill, and speedily expelling them from this position, compelled them to seek refuge in the mill and houses. Lieutenant Johnson then attempted to storm one of the houses filled with brigands, and in the act of doing so was killed, and four rank and file wounded. Being destitute of artillery to batter the houses, the party was ordered to retire. In this affair the brigands sustained a loss of about 40 killed and 28 prisoners.

On the 16th of this month, Colonel Dundas and four companies of the regiment, with some heavy artillery, landed at Prescott, and at once took up position about 500 yards from the mill. The guns were brought to bear on the houses with great effect, and it being now late, and daylight wearing away, the lieutenant-colonel ordered the regiment to advance, when a smart fire was opened by the brigands from one of the houses, and as quickly replied to. The buildings on the left of the mill being by this time gained, were set fire to, and the enemy, seeing no prospect of escape, threw out a "white flag," and about 130 of them surrendered unconditionally.

Their killed in this affair amounted to about 30. The only loss sustained by the regiment on this occasion was one private killed. The four companies returned to Kingston the day following.

1839. During this year the regiment remained stationary at Kingston.

1840. On the 19th May, 1840, the officer named in the margin [1] died at this station, and he was

---

[1] Lieutenant and Adjutant J. Stubbs.

succeeded first by Lieutenant B. H. Browne, and on his promotion Ensign William Nott was appointed adjutant. Ensign Nott was promoted from the ranks, and performed the duties of adjutant most efficiently for eleven years, when he became captain by seniority in 1851, at Kurrachee.

The regiment remained at Kingston, N.S., until the 20th and 21st May, 1840, when it embarked in steamboats for London and St. Thomas, N.S., and marched into quarters at these stations on the 29th and 30th of the same month.

1841. On the 14th May, 1841, Lieutenant Wynniatt was accidentally drowned while endeavouring to ford the River Thomas on horseback.

On the 4th October, 1841, Captain Colquhoun died at London (England) while on leave of absence.

1842. The 1st division of the regiment, under the command of Brevet Major Swinburne, marched *en route* to Toronto on the 7th July, 1842; and the 2nd division or head-quarters, under the command of Lieutenant-Colonel Trydell, on the following day. The former arrived at Toronto on the 14th, and the latter on the 15th July, 1842.

On the 2nd August, 1842, Brevet Lieutenant-Colonel B. Trydell succeeded to the lieutenant-colonelcy of the regiment, vice the Hon. H. Dundas, placed on half-pay.

1843. The 1st division of the regiment proceeded on the 22nd May, 1843, to Three Rivers, under the command of Major Swinburne. The 2nd division and head-quarters proceeded to Quebec on the 23rd, and arrived there on the 27th May. No. 4 company joined head-quarters at Quebec on the 30th May, leaving No. 1 and the Light Company at Three Rivers. Light

Company and No. 1 joined the head-quarters at Quebec on the 11th June, 1843, from Three Rivers.[1]

The regiment embarked for England at Quebec, Canada, on the 16th June, 1843. The 1st division and head-quarters, under the command of Lieutenant-Colonel Trydell, on board the *Countess*, London freight ship, consisting of 3 captains, 5 subalterns, 3 staff, 28 sergeants, 8 drummers, and 502 rank and file, 54 women, and 110 children; and the 2nd division, under the command of Major Swinburne, on board the *Jamaica*, freight ship, consisting of 1 captain, 4 subalterns, 1 staff, 10 sergeants, 2 drummers, 184 rank and file, 16 women, and 20 children, sailed together on the 17th June, 1843, and both ships anchored at Spithead on the 10th July, 1843.

The 2nd division, under the command of Major Swinburne, landed at Gosport on the 11th; and the 1st division and head-quarters, under the command of Lieutenant-Colonel Trydell, on the 12th July, 1843.

The regiment was quartered in Forton Barracks, Gosport, until the 17th July, when the 1st division proceeded by railroad, through London, to Weedon, and the head-quarters division on the following day, at which they occupied barracks until the 4th August, 1843, when the head-quarters with two companies proceeded to Northampton, and the remainder of the regiment was distributed in detachments at Birmingham, Wolverhampton, Burslem, Coventry, Hanley, and Newcastle-under-Lyme.

On the 17th October, 1843, the regiment received the new percussion muskets.

1844. In April, 1844, the regiment was again collected at Weedon, where it remained till October,

[1] The regiment, on its route from Toronto to Quebec, passed down the Lachine Rapids, in the River St. Lawrence; the 1st division on the 23rd, and the 2nd division on the 24th May, 1843.

1844, when the head-quarters and three companies proceeded to Leeds, and the remainder furnished detachments to York, Bradford, Sheffield, Keighley, Huddersfield, Halifax, and Scarborough Castle.

1845. In June, 1845, the regiment was assembled at Manchester, where it remained till 22nd July, when it proceeded by rail to Liverpool, and embarked for Dublin, where it arrived the following morning, and proceeded *en route* to Limerick, Cahir, and Tipperary. The head-quarters of the regiment were established at Limerick, and furnished detachments also to Kilrush, the forts on the Shannon, Rathkeale, Newcastle, Castleconnell, Croom, Ennis, and Clare Castle.

1846. In September, 1846, the regiment proceeded by divisions to Dublin, and was assembled there in October. It occupied Richmond Barracks, and subsequently detached companies to Aldboro' House and Island Bridge Barracks.

During the stay of the regiment at Dublin, Captain T. J. St. Aubyn died while on leave of absence in Surrey.

1847. In May, 1847, the head-quarters proceeded to Kilkenny, and during its stay there furnished detachments to Carlow, Castlecomer, Carrick-on-Suir, Bagenalstown, Thomas Town, Wexford, Enniscarthy, New Ross, Callan, and Graignenemagh.

1848. Lieutenant T. Lane died at Castlecomer on 26th June, 1848.

On the 1st September, 1848, Major-General Sir Frederick Stovin, K.C.B. and K.C.M.G., succeeded General Frazer in the colonelcy of the regiment.

In September, 1848, the regiment was removed to Fermoy, whence it furnished detachments to Fethard, Lismore, and Clogheen.

PART V

SERVICES OF THE REGIMENT IN INDIA, 1849-57

ON the 1st December, 1848, the regiment was ordered to be augmented to the establishment as per margin,[1] and received instructions to prepare for service in the East Indies, and on the 9th January, 1849, two companies, with head-quarters, proceeded to Cork, and embarked on the 11th, under the command of Lieutenant-Colonel Trydell, in the freight ship *Bombay*, for Bombay, and sailed for its destination on the 17th of the same month.

1849. The remainder of the regiment followed in the succeeding months of February and March, as follows, viz.—

In the *China*, under Major Townsend.
In the *Mermaid*, under Brevet Major Ainslie.
In the *Marion*, under Lieutenant-Colonel Law.
In the *Ursula*, under Captain Lloyd.
In the *Zion's Hope*, under Major Swinburne.

On the 8th May, 1849, the head-quarters arrived in Bombay, and on the 10th, disembarked and proceeded to Poona, and arrived at that station on the 18th of the same month. The whole of the regiment, however, was not assembled at Poona till the 14th July, 1849, where it remained till November, 1850.

During the stay of the regiment at Poona, it lost by disease two officers (Captain the Hon. W. Gage and

---

[1] Officers, 52 ; non-commissioned and rank and file, 1079 ; total 1131.

Surgeon Ledingham), 5 sergeants, 1 drummer, and 69 rank and file.

1850 In November, 1850, the regiment marched in four divisions on the 2nd, 3rd, 4th, and 11th of the month for Panwell and Bombay, and embarked in steamers for Kurrachee, where the head-quarters arrived and disembarked on the 14th of the same month, but the last division did not join the regiment till the 1st December following.

1851. In January, 1851, Lieutenant-Colonel Trydell was appointed to the command of the Poona brigade, and Lieutenant-Colonel W. H. Law assumed command of the regiment.

From November, 1850, to 31st December, 1852, the regiment was stationed at Kurrachee, and lost through disease during that period 5 officers—viz., Major Townsend, Lieutenant and Adjutant W. Hall,[1] Ensign Graham, Quartermaster Colburn (at Poona when on leave), and Assistant-Surgeon Boyce—and 6 sergeants, 3 drummers, and 135 rank and file, chiefly cases of cholera, fever, and dysentery.

On two occasions—viz., in May and June, 1851, and again in September and October, 1852—the regiment was visited with cholera, fever, and dysentery, and suffered greatly, and on the last occasion it was considered necessary to remove the regiment from the barracks and encamp the men on Ghizree Heights, near the sea.[2]

1852. It, however, soon recovered from these fell diseases, and numbered upwards of 950 efficient soldiers, men strong and stalwart in form, perfect in

---

[1] Lieutenant W. Hall became adjutant in April, but died very soon afterwards. He had been promoted from the ranks. He was succeeded as adjutant by Lieutenant E. H. M. Mainwaring.

[2] The 64th Regiment were quartered with the 83rd during the time they were in Kurrachee, and the two regiments were on the most friendly terms from being so much together.

discipline, and influenced in no ordinary degree by an ardent *esprit de corps*, the prestige of the honourable name and high reputation won by the 83rd wherever it served.

1853. On the 8th February, the right wing of the regiment (448 strength), under the command of Brevet Lieutenant-Colonel Swinburne, proceeded in river steamers by the Indus River to Hyderabad, there to be stationed.

On the 15th March, 1853, the establishment of the regiment was altered by Horse Guards' letter, dated 24th March, 1853, to 12 captains, 20 lieutenants, 4 ensigns, and 1 adjutant.

Brevet Lieutenant-Colonel Joseph Swinburne, after a long and distinguished service of forty-four years in the 83rd Regiment, retired from the service on the full pay of his rank of major. He served throughout the whole of the Peninsular campaign (the greater part of the time as adjutant), and received a medal and ten clasps for Talavera, Busaco, Fuentes d'Onor, Ciudad Rodrigo, Badajoz, Salamanca, Vittoria, Nivelle, Orthes, Toulouse. He was engaged with the regiment in the Kandyan rebellion and in Canada, and, embarking with the regiment for India, left it on the 22nd May, 1853, with the esteem and veneration of every individual in it.

He was succeeded in the majority by Captain Henry Lloyd.

The head-quarters, consisting of 5 subalterns, 4 staff, 19 sergeants, 6 drummers, and 353 rank and file, embarked at Kurrachee on board the Hon. E. I. C. steam frigate *Semiramis*, for Gogo, *en route* for Deesa; landed at Gogo on the 22nd December, where they were halted and encamped awaiting further orders.

On the departure of head-quarters from Scinde, Major-General Sir Henry Somerset, K.C.B., issued a very complimentary order to the regiment. Lieutenant-Colonel W. H. Law was then commanding, and Lieutenant E. H. M. Mainwaring was adjutant.

1854. On the 9th January, 1854, Major Henry Lloyd joined from England, and assumed command of the head-quarters division at Gogo, Guzerat.

On the 22nd January, 1854, the head-quarters division, under Major Lloyd, marched from Gogo, and arrived at Deesa on the 13th February.

On the 23rd April, Major Henry Lloyd made over command of the head-quarters division to Captain E. W. Bray, the senior officer, and left Deesa for Kurrachee, there to assume command of the right wing.

On the 6th May, Major Henry Lloyd died at Cambay of Asiatic cholera, while proceeding by that route to Kurrachee, to assume command of the companies there stationed.

On the 14th October, the half-yearly inspection of the head-quarters division of the regiment took place at Camp Deesa, under Brigadier-General Forster Stalker, C.B., commanding northern division of the army. Captain E. W. Bray at that time commanded, and Lieutenant E. H. M. Mainwaring was adjutant.

1855. On the 4th January, Colonel W. H. Law joined from Kurrachee, and assumed command of the head-quarters division of the regiment stationed at Deesa.

On the 29th March, the half-yearly inspection of the head-quarters division of the regiment took place at Camp Deesa, under Major-General F. Stalker, C.B., commanding northern division of the army.

On the 2nd April, the right wing, consisting of seven companies, under the command of Captain C. W. Austen, arrived at Bombay, from Kurrachee, and was quartered in the barracks of Colaba.

During its service in Scinde the regiment lost through disease, 5 officers, 6 sergeants, 4 drummers, 142 rank and file.

On the 9th March, a draft, consisting of 1 sergeant, 2 corporals, and 35 privates, under the command of Ensign G. Mylne, joined the head-quarters of the regiment at Deesa from England.

On the 29th October, the half-yearly inspection of the head-quarters division of the regiment took place under Major-General F. Stalker, C.B., commanding northern division of the army.

On the morning of the 22nd December, the right wing of the regiment, consisting of seven companies (strength—1 field officer, 2 captains, 4 subalterns, 20 sergeants, 8 drummers, 477 rank and file), under the command of Major Kelsall, embarked at Bombay on board of the *Ajdaha* for Domus, where it disembarked on the following day, and on the 25th commenced its march upon Deesa, viâ Surat, Baroda, and Ahmedabad, and finally reached its destination on the 25th January, 1856, after having been separated from head-quarters for a period of three years.

1856. On the 21st January, an order was received to hold a wing of the regiment in readiness to proceed on field service.

On the 30th of the same month. 42 recruits, under the command of Lieutenant Cooper, joined the regiment from England.

On the 27th March, the half-yearly inspection of the regiment took place, under Brigadier N. Wilson, K.H., commanding Deesa Field Brigade.

On 16th May, Colonel W. H. Law retired on full pay from the service, with the rank of major-general; he served in the Peninsular War, and was present at the battles of Nivelle and Nive, for which he received the war medal and two clasps. Colonel Trydell being brigadier at Poona, the command of the regiment devolved on Lieutenant-Colonel Kelsall, the second lieutenant-colonel.

On the 1st August, Lieutenant and Adjutant E. H. M. Mainwaring died at Poona.

On the 27th October the half-yearly inspection of the regiment took place, under Brigadier N. Wilson, K.H., commanding Deesa Field Brigade.

1857. On the 23rd March a detachment, in strength 3 sergeants, 4 drummers, 9 rank and file, 6 women, and 15 children, proceeded, under the command of Lieutenant Dickenson (and in medical charge of Assistant-Surgeon Miles), to Mount Aboo.

During the month of May, 1857, the regiment was held in readiness for field service, in consequence of the mutinies of the Bengal native army; and on the 26th of that month the left wing, composed of Nos. 5, 6, 7, and the Light Company (strength—1 field officer, 2 captains, 6 subalterns, 2 staff, 18 sergeants, 6 drummers, 250 rank and file), under the command of Major Steele, proceeded on active service and marched on Nusseerabad, where it arrived on the 12th June, having performed a march of 237 miles in seventeen days during the hottest time of the year without a single casualty.

On the 13th June No. 7 Company was detached from the left wing to garrison the fort and arsenal of Ajmere.

The left wing was reinforced by Nos. 1, 2, 3 Companies (strength—1 captain, 2 subalterns, 7 sergeants, 3 drummers, 200 rank and file), which left the headquarters at Deesa on the 17th June, and arrived at Nusseerabad on the 10th July.

On the 9th July two companies, under the command

of Captain Read, were detached from Nusseerabad to Neemuch, 143 miles distant, where they arrived on the 18th of the same month.

On the 14th July the Grenadier Company, under the command of Captain Jones, left head-quarters for Ahmedabad, the native troops in garrison there having displayed symptoms of disaffection.

On the 10th August the left wing at Nusseerabad disarmed a detachment of the 12th Regiment N.I., which had exhibited evident symptoms of a mutinous spirit; and on the night of the 12th of the same month, the detachment at Neemuch, under Captain S. Read, was called out to suppress a mutiny of a squadron of the 2nd Bombay Light Cavalry; the night was exceedingly dark, but the detachment succeeded in making several prisoners, and sustained a loss of one man killed (Private Chambers) and two wounded.

On the 21st August the detachment of the 50 invalids at Mount Aboo was attacked by about 150 mutineers of the Joudpoor Legion, who were repulsed with some loss in killed and wounded, without the detachment having sustained any loss. On receipt of this intelligence at Nusseerabad, a wing of the Joudpoor Legion, there stationed, was disarmed by the 83rd Regiment.

On the 30th August a detachment of 3 officers and 119 rank and file, under the command of Brevet Major Heatly, proceeded from Nusseerabad for the purpose of preserving the peace of the city of Ajmere during a Mohammedan festival. This detachment was joined on the 1st September by a detail of 1 sergeant and 30 rank and file from the company stationed in the fort of Ajmere. The detachment then proceeded on active service to Beawar, where it was reinforced by

1 captain, 2 sergeants, 1 drummer, and 50 rank and file from Nusseerabad; the detachment then, with four guns of the Bombay Horse Artillery and some native troops, proceeded by the mountain pass of Burr, on a reconnaissance to Awah, which they found to be a strongly entrenched village, garrisoned by about 3000 armed men, well provided with artillery. On the 18th September an unsuccessful attack was made on the village, in which three men, 83rd Regiment, were wounded, two of our four guns were disabled, and one artilleryman was killed and two wounded, and some casualties occurred amongst our native troops; the whole force then returned to Ajmere, where it arrived on the 28th September.

On the night of the 18th September the detachment stationed at Neemuch, under the command of Captain Read, together with two guns supported by a detail of native troops, marched from Neemuch to take the walled village of Nimbhera, sixteen miles distant, which was occupied by mutineers and rebels with three guns; during the following day the force took up a position near the village, and opened fire with the view of effecting a breach; the fire was kept up till dark, when further operations were suspended till next day. During the night of the 19th the enemy, leaving their guns, ammunition, etc., hastily evacuated the village, which was taken possession of by the force on the morning of the 20th.

During the action of the 19th Assistant-Surgeon Miles was wounded in the leg, and Lance-Corporal Thomas Young was killed.

On this occasion each man of the detachment received 8 rupees (16s.) prize-money. On the night of the 20th September the force returned to Neemuch, leaving 1 sergeant, 1 drummer, and 30 rank and file, under

Ensign Chamley, to occupy the village, which detachment rejoined the following day.[1]

A considerable body of the Mundisore insurgents having occupied the fort and village of Jeerun, about ten miles from Neemuch, on the morning of the 23rd October a detachment of 50 of the 83rd, commanded by Captain Read, together with a company of the 12th Bombay N.I., some native cavalry, and two guns, moved against them from Neemuch. A very determined resistance was offered by the enemy, and Captain Read was killed by one of their first musket shots, while leading on his small detachment. Captain Tucker commanding the cavalry was killed, and the officer commanding the native infantry detachment was severely wounded about the same time. The enemy advancing in great force, the infantry retired to a fresh position, and the enemy having suffered severely from their fire, withdrew into the fort of Jeerun, which was occupied and blown up on the following morning, the enemy having evacuated it in the night. In addition to the death of Captain Read, two privates were wounded in this affair.

On the 9th November the small fortified position at Neemuch, which was garrisoned by a detachment of the 83rd Regiment, under Ensign Chamley, and some native troops, the whole under command of Major Simpson, 2nd Light Cavalry, was attacked by a very large insurgent force, which invested the fortification for fifteen days; their several attempts at assault by escalade were repulsed with heavy loss, and on the 23rd of the month they broke up and retired on the advance of a force from Mhow to the relief of the garrison, which had sustained a loss of about 20 in wounded during the siege.

[1] On the 4th October, 1857, Captain R. C. Jones died at Ahmedabad.

The head-quarters of the regiment, which had remained at Deesa up to this time, received orders to advance into Rajpootana, and marched for Mount Aboo on the 26th October, under command of Colonel Trydell; thence it proceeded to Nusseerabad, where it arrived on the 28th November.

The detachment at Neemuch was now relieved by two companies commanded by Major Austen.

PART VI

SERVICES OF THE REGIMENT, 1858-63

1858. AN expedition was organized for the reduction of the fortress of Awah, and two companies of the regiment having joined it, about 1000 men of all arms, with some siege guns, arrived before Awah on the 19th January.

Batteries were constructed, and their fire was warmly replied to by the enemy; an assault was arranged for the morning of the 24th January, but, favoured by a night of intense darkness and a heavy thunderstorm, the enemy evacuated the fortress during the night of the 23rd, about 50 of their number being killed, or taken by the picquets. Thirteen guns were taken in the place. The defences and fortified palace were mined and destroyed. The detachment had two men wounded.

Colonel Trydell and Lieutenant-Colonel Kelsall having proceeded to England, the command of the regiment devolved on Major Steele on the 24th February, 1858.

On the 8th March the regiment was joined by a draft of 152 men from England commanded by Captain Wright.

SIEGE AND CAPTURE OF KOTAH

The strongly fortified city of Kotah on the River Chumbul had been for many months held by a formidable insurgent force. Major-General Roberts, of the Honourable East India Company's Army, commanding in Rajpootana, now moved against it from Nusseerabad, with two strong brigades; the 1st marching on the 10th March. With this brigade were three companies of the regiment, under the command of Captain (Brevet Lieutenant-Colonel) Heatly.

The 2nd Brigade, commanded by Colonel Parke, of the 72nd Highlanders, to which the head-quarters of the regiment (strength 11 officers and 300 men) was attached, moved from Nusseerabad on the 11th March. The whole force comprised H.M.'s 8th Hussars, a company of Royal Engineers, the 72nd, 83rd, and 95th Regiments, a numerous force of native cavalry and infantry, a siege-train of 18 heavy guns and mortars, also 3 troops and batteries of horse and foot artillery of the Hon. Company's service—about 4500 of all arms. The force encamped on the 22nd March before the city, on the opposite bank of the River Chumbul; the regiment furnished the usual working parties, trench and battery guards, outlying picquets, etc., until the 25th of the month, when, the capture by the enemy of the Rajah's palace, which was held by our troops, being imminent, 200 men of the detachment of H.M.'s 83rd Regiment, with the 1st Brigade, were directed to cross the river, with other troops, for its protection; this detachment sustained a loss of 3 men killed and 5 non-commissioned officers and men wounded in the following three days, in which some vigorous assaults by the enemy were repulsed with heavy loss in killed and wounded. On the 30th the city was taken, having been entered by three columns of assault, the centre column being led by the head-quarters division of the 83rd Regiment, under Lieutenant-Colonel Steele; the detachment of the 83rd with the 1st Brigade, commanded by Brevet Lieutenant-Colonel Heatly, was in reserve, and entered the city later in the day. The regiment sustained a loss of 1 man killed and 6 wounded. The enemy abandoned their defences and retired towards Gwalior, having sustained a considerable loss in the siege and assault; about 80 guns were taken in the city, with large magazines of ammunition and supplies.

Having remained encamped before Kotah till the 18th April, the besieging force was broken up, and the regiment marched on return to Nusseerabad, arriving there on the 29th. The usual relief of detachment of one company in the fort of Ajmere took place on the 3rd May.

Enfield rifles were issued to the regiment at this time; the waist-belt, with small pouch in front, had been supplied to the regiment in supercession of the old cross-belts about one year previously.

Lieutenant-Colonel Kelsall having retired on full pay, Major Steele succeeded to the rank of Lieutenant-Colonel of the regiment on the 13th April, 1858.

On the 23rd May, the two companies which had been on detachment at Neemuch, under command of Major Austen, since December, rejoined the head-quarters of the regiment.

About the middle of June, the decisive successes of the division of the army commanded by Major-General H. Rose having caused the rebel army to evacuate the Gwalior territory, a very numerous hostile force, estimated at 10,000 men, crossed the River Chumbul, and entered the territory of the Rajah of Jeypoor, who had always displayed friendly feelings towards the British Government. A considerable force, about 2500 strong, of which the head-quarters and 600 of the 83rd composed a part, was placed under orders for field service in consequence, and marched from Nusseerabad on the 28th June, under command of Major-General Roberts. On the 3rd July this force arrived within one march of the city of Jeypoor, which was in imminent danger from the advance of the rebel army. On the approach of General Roberts's division, the enemy, changing their direction, moved southwards and attacked the capital of the Rajah of Tonk, which was occupied and partially plundered by them The Rajah retired to his fortified palace, and offered all the resistance in his power to their assaults. A portion of his troops, however, proved faithless, and joined the enemy, giving up to them the guns which had been in their charge.

General Roberts's advance by forced marches caused the rebels to retire from before Tonk, and a considerable portion of the British force was detached in pursuit in a south-easterly direction; about 900 men, including the 83rd Regiment, remaining under the personal command of the general. The weather was at this time extremely hot, and the exposure consequent on the urgent duties in which the force was engaged proved fatal to many of the soldiers composing it. Six men of the 83rd died from sunstroke between the 7th and 10th July.

The enemy, pressed upon by the detached column, changed their line of march towards the west, and General Roberts, still moving by forced marches, succeeded in coming up with them late on the evening of the 8th August. They were seen formed in great force near the village of Sanganeer—the number was estimated at 8000 men, two-thirds of whom were cavalry. The regiment at once advanced to the attack under a heavy fire from the artillery of the enemy, which, however, being directed too high, did no execution, while many of the rebels were killed and wounded by the rifles of the 83rd. Darkness, however, coming on, enabled the enemy to retire and withdraw the whole of their guns. The force had marched this day thirty miles, and bivouacked on the spot, having far outmarched their tents and baggage. Waiting one day to allow the column which had been detached from Tonk to join him, General Roberts's force moved on the 10th August in pursuit of the enemy. This brigade had been reinforced by the junction of one troop of Bombay Horse Artillery, a squadron of the 8th Royal Irish Hussars, a squadron of Native Light Cavalry, 4 companies 72nd Highlanders, and a Sepoy Regiment of the Bombay army, as well as by a strong body of Belooch horsemen.

A very persevering pursuit now took place on the track of the rebel army, the outpost picquets of which were surprised and cut to pieces on more than one occasion. At about 7 a.m. on the 14th August, the enemy were seen moving in heavy masses, of horse and foot, on the further bank of the Bunnass River, their line of movement being covered by their artillery, which was posted in a battery on the crest of a rising ground close to the village of Kottaria; only waiting to form and load, the force at once advanced towards the river, the 83rd Regiment leading in a double column of sub-divisions from its centre. The enemy's guns opened with round and grape, and were instantly vigorously engaged by the British Horse Artillery, and the fire on both sides was for a time extremely heavy. The 83rd, forming line, crossed the river, meeting but little resistance, and the enemy, abandoning their guns, retired with precipitation. The cavalry charged amongst the retreating artillerymen and infantry, and the pursuit was continued for some miles, very great numbers of the rebels falling under their sabres, while the fugitives seeking shelter in the groves and copse-wood were destroyed by our infantry. In the evening the force returned and encamped near Kottaria, having sustained only the small loss of 22 killed and wounded, while fully 1000 of the rebels were left dead on the field, and 4 guns, with their ammunition, and many elephants and camels laden with stores, were captured. The enemy's flight did not cease till they had crossed the Chumbul and entirely evacuated Rajpootana. The force returned northwards by easy marches, and the regiment reoccupied its former quarters in the camp at Nusseerabad on the 29th of August.

On the 4th October the first half-yearly inspection of the regiment which had taken place since April, 1857, was made by Major-General Roberts, commanding Rajpootana Field Force, who was pleased to issue a highly complimentary order to the regiment on this occasion. Lieutenant-Colonel Steele was commanding and Lieutenant J. N. Colthurst was adjutant.

1858. By order of her Majesty, published 18th August, 1858, a medal and clasp was granted to all the troops engaged in field service in the repression of the mutinies in India, and lists of those so entitled in the regiment were forwarded on the 3rd and 4th November, 1858.

By order of the Governor-General in Council, dated 29th September, 1858, a donation of six months' full batta was granted to all officers and men who had served with the Rajpootana Field Force.

On October 26th, 1858, Colonel Botet Trydell was promoted to major-general, and Major C. W. Austen succeeded to the lieutenant-colonelcy in the regiment.

Major-General Trydell served in the 83rd for a period of fifty-four years. He was present with the 1st Battalion at the taking of the Cape of Good Hope in 1806, including the battle of Blueberg; and also in Ceylon through the Kandyan rebellion.

Lieutenant-Colonel Steele having proceeded to England early in the month of December, 1858, the command of the regiment devolved on Lieutenant-Colonel Austen, the second lieutenant-colonel. On the 17th of this month, a field force was formed at Nusseerabad under the personal command of Brigadier Honner, commanding Rajpootana Field Force, consisting of the head-quarters of the 83rd Regiment, 500 strong, under command of Lieutenant-Colonel C. Austen, with a troop and a half-battery of artillery, a considerable force of cavalry of the 8th Hussars and 1st Lancers, and the 12th Regiment N.I. The force marched to Sanganeer on the Neemuch road, arriving there on the 21st. On the 23rd the head-quarters of the 83rd, 300 strong, with the 12th Regiment N.I., and half a battery, were ordered back to Nusseerabad, arriving there on the 27th. Three companies under Lieutenant-Colonel Heatly, consisting of 200 men, remained with the brigade under Brigadier Honner.

1859. Early in the month of January, 1859, intelligence having been received that the rebel force was again moving on Tonk, with the intention of reaching Jeypoor, the head-quarters of the 83rd, with 300 men, part of the 12th Regiment N.I., and half a battery of artillery, the whole under the command of Lieutenant-Colonel Holmes, proceeded on the 8th in an easterly direction to Diggee, to cover the road from Tonk to Jeypoor. Having received information that Tonk was threatened, the force marched through Tonk to Bamboor on the 11th; here it was discovered that the rebels had passed by, and the force accordingly marched the following day (twenty-two miles) in a north-east route to Jullai. Finding that the rebels had only left that morning, and were encamped at Chatsoo, twenty-two miles distant, the force marched again that night, arriving at Chatsoo before daybreak. The rebels had just left when the brigade of Brigadier Showers—chiefly cavalry — having come up, continued the pursuit. Colonel Holmes's force then marched on Jeypoor, arriving there on the 17th and leaving on the 18th, and after four days' severe marching through deep sand, came up with the rebel force at "Seekur" at 4 a.m., having during the last thirty hours accomplished a march of fifty-two miles. The moon was just setting when our troops surprised the rebel camp, and owing to the darkness and precipitation with which the rebels fled, together with our deficiency of cavalry, our troops were unable to inflict any serious loss on them. About 80 were killed, 50 taken prisoners, and many horses and camels. The force halted at Seekur for one day, having during the previous thirteen days marched a distance of 292 miles. After this, the force proceeded in combination with other columns to harass the rebels, and marched over a great part of Jeypoor and Joudpoor, arriving finally on the 18th February at Suget on the road between Nusseerabad and Deesa. Information having been here received that the rebels had escaped through a pass in the hills, the force, after a halt of four days, returned to Nusseerabad, arriving there on the 1st March.

The field force, under Brigadier Honner, to which were attached 200 men of the 83rd Regiment, under Lieutenant-Colonel Heatly, also returned on the 1st March, having been in the field since the 14th December, during which period they traversed 995 miles of country; and on one occasion, in attempting to surprise the rebels, they marched forty-four miles in twenty-four hours. In the pursuit of the rebels, terminating in the affair of Kosana, Brigadier Honner's force marched 130 miles, over tracts of deep, heavy land, in four days. The 83rd detachment in this last pursuit, consisting of 9 sergeants, 4 corporals, 1 drummer, and 119 privates, under command of Lieutenant-Colonel Heatly, with Captain Marsh, Lieutenants Onslow and Huyshe, were mounted on camels. Their services during the operations terminating in the defeat of the rebels at "Koshana" are honourably mentioned in Brigadier Honner's despatch.

In the summer of 1859 a letter was addressed by the Earl of Howth, Lord-Lieutenant of the county of Dublin, to General Sir Frederick Stovin, G.C.B. and K.C.M.G., the colonel of the regiment, which is subjoined:—

"HOWTH CASTLE, *July 28th,* 1859.

"SIR,—An application has been made to me by Lieutenant-Colonel Steele, of the 83rd Regiment, in my capacity of the Lord-Lieutenant of the county of Dublin, to give the assistance of my sanction and co-operation in forwarding an application from him as commanding officer of the 83rd Regiment, that the distinctive appellation of the 'County of Dublin' Regiment may be conferred upon that corps. Lieutenant-Colonel Steele has suggested that I should communicate with you as the colonel of the 83rd on the subject of his wishes, and I accordingly beg to do so. Lieutenant-Colonel Steele accompanied his application to me by an extract from the records of the 83rd Regiment, and it most plainly appears that the regiment was raised in the county of Dublin in the year 1793, under a letter of service granted to its first lientenant-colonel commandant, William Fitch, who was killed at the head of the regiment in the Maroon war, in the island of Jamaica, three years afterwards. It further appears from its records that the 83rd Regiment has seen much active foreign service, and has been distinguished by its discipline and valour in many parts of the world, and recently in the suppression of the mutiny in India, where it is at present serving.

"Under these circumstances, and having regard to the fact that the regiment was originally raised exclusively in the county of Dublin, I have much pleasure in expressing my concurrence in the application made by Lieutenant-Colonel Steele on the part of his regiment. I consider that it would be creditable to the county of Dublin, that a regiment raised in it, and of whose services it may be very justly proud, should be distinguished by its name, and I give this letter to Lieutenant-Colonel Steele for conveyance to you, in the hope that it may aid in inducing his

Royal Highness the Commander-in-Chief to recommend to her Majesty that the title of the 'County of Dublin' Regiment may be conferred on the 83rd.

"I have the honour, etc.,
"(Signed)   HOWTH.

"To General Sir F. Stovin, G.C.B. and K.C.M.G.,
  Colonel 83rd Regiment."

This application was brought to the notice of his Royal Highness the Duke of Cambridge, Commander-in-Chief of the Army, by Sir F. Stovin, and the title of the "County of Dublin" Regiment was conferred on the 83rd.

The following letter from the Adjutant-General reached the regiment at Nusseerabad on the 19th December, 1859, just sixty-seven years after the regiment had been raised in the county of Dublin :—

"HORSE GUARDS, S.W., *October 29th*, 1859.

"SIR,—By desire of his Royal Highness the General Commanding-in-Chief, I have the honour to acquaint you that her Majesty has been graciously pleased to authorize the 83rd Regiment, which was raised principally from recruits obtained in Ireland in 1793, and embodied in Dublin in that year, being designated the 83rd (County of Dublin) Regiment.

"I have the honour, etc.,
"(Signed)   W. F. FORSTER, D.A.-Gen."

1860. The regiment remained at Nusseerabad and Ajmere till the end of February, 1860, when they were ordered to proceed to Belgaum, in the southern Mahratta country; and the head-quarters division, commanded by Lieutenant-Colonel Austen, marched on the 17th February, reached Cambay, distant 390 miles, on the 30th March, and proceeded by sea to Vingorla, on the Malabar coast, whence they marched to Belgaum, arriving there on the 16th April.

The left wing moved on the 30th March, under command of Captain Baumgartner, and had a trying march in very hot weather, during which they lost an officer (Lieutenant Colebrook) and several men from cholera.

They proceeded from Cambay by sea to Wagotna, and marched to Kolapore, where they remained on detachment under command of Captain E. B. Cooke.

A highly complimentary farewell order was issued to the regiment on the occasion of its ceasing to belong to the Rajpootana Field Force, by Brigadier Honner, C.B., commanding in Malwa and Rajpootana. Lieutenant-Colonel Austen was then in command of the regiment.

The half-yearly inspection of the regiment was made by Brigadier Adams, C.B., commanding the southern Mahratta division, on the 7th November, 1860, at Belgaum.

The wing of the regiment which had been on detachment at Kolapore since May, 1860, joined head-quarters on November 27th, 1860.

1861. The medals awarded by her Majesty to the officers and men who had been engaged with the enemy during the Indian Mutiny were received from the Adjutant-General, Horse Guards, on 2nd February, 1861, and on 11th February they were presented to those entitled to them on a parade of the garrison of Belgaum by Miss Straith, the step-daughter of the brigadier commanding.

The officers of the regiment who were presented with the Indian war medal were:—

Lieut.-Col. Steele, C.B.	Lieutenant Wardell.
Lieut.-Col. Heatly.	Lieutenant Onslow.
Captain Pigott.	Lieutenant Karslake.
Lieut.-Col. C. W. Austen.	Lieutenant Healy.
Captain Wright.	Lieutenant Coote.
Captain Wakefield.	Lieutenant Beazley.
Captain Minhear.	Lieutenant Huyshe.
Captain Meurant.	Lieutenant Pennefather.
Captain Baumgartner.	Lieutenant Anderson.
Captain Gandy.	Paymaster Swinburne.
Captain Gore.	Assistant-Surgeon Touch.
Captain Molony.	Assistant-Surgeon W. Sharp.
Adjutant J. N. Colthurst.	Quartermaster Hayes.
Lieutenant Browne.	Captain Sprot.

Lieutenant-Colonel Steele, who had commanded the regiment in several engagements in the early part of the Mutiny, had been decorated by her Majesty with the insignia of a Companion of the Bath for his services.

The half-yearly inspection of the regiment was made by Brigadier Adams, C.B., commanding the southern Mahratta division on April 25th, 1861.

A frock of scarlet serge, and a wicker helmet covered with grey linen, with a turban round it, were ordered to be adopted by the regiments in India, in supersession of the shell jacket and chaco hitherto worn, and the regiment was provided with them accordingly about this time.

Intimation was received in August that the regiment was to embark for England in the approaching cold season. On the 18th November, his Excellency Lieutenant-General Sir William Mansfield, K.C.B., Commander-in-Chief of the Bombay presidency, having visited Belgaum on a tour of inspection, went through the barracks of the regiment, and afterwards reviewed the 83rd on a brigade field-day, at the conclusion of which he was pleased to make a speech to the regiment, in which he expressed his approbation of the state of the corps in the strongest terms; his Excellency used the words that "he never in the course of his service had seen a regiment in higher order, and that he should not fail to report accordingly to his Royal Highness the Commander-in-Chief."

Immediately afterwards the regiment was permitted by general order to give volunteers for further service in India to every regiment serving there, and a number of non-commissioned officers and men, as per margin,[1] having volunteered to other regiments, were struck off the strength of the 83rd from the 19th December, 1861.

[1] Sergeants, 8; corporals, 10; drummers, 7; privates, 463.

1862. The regiment commenced its march to the coast on the 22nd January, 1862, and reached Vingorla on the 29th of that month, where they were encamped till the 5th of February, on which day the regiment, under command of Lieutenant-Colonel Steele, C.B., embarked in the hired transport *King Lear;* the ship sailed the same evening for Plymouth.

During the service of the regiment in India of $12\frac{1}{2}$ years, it lost by deaths 18 officers, 30 sergeants, 417 rank and file; and 51 sergeants and 629 rank and file were invalided.

The *King Lear* anchored in Table Bay, Cape of Good Hope, on the morning of the 18th March, and having obtained supplies sailed again for Gravesend, where the regiment disembarked on the 21st May, 1862, and proceeded to Dover on the same day by rail, and was quartered in the citadel.

The regiment was soon afterwards inspected by Brigadier-General Garvock, commanding at Dover, and by Major-General Hon. A. A. Dalzell, commanding the division.

Lieutenant-Colonel Edward Steele, C.B., sold out of the regiment on the 29th July, after a service of twenty-eight years in the 83rd. He died in London on the 6th August, only eight days after he had been gazetted out.

Major A. Barnard Hankey succeeded to the lieutenant-colonelcy of the regiment.

In August the regiment was reviewed by Lieutenant-General Viscount Melville, K.C.B., who commanded it for several years in Canada and England.

Several drafts of recruits, both officers and men, joined head-quarters from the depôt at Chatham, and brought up the strength of the regiment, which had been reduced to a mere skeleton by the volunteering at Belgaum, and the discharge of many men on its arrival at Dover.

In October the regiment was inspected on the Castle Hill parade ground by H.R.H. the Duke of Cambridge, Commander-in-Chief, who, in a complimentary speech, expressed his approval of its appearance, and of the rapid manner in which the regiment had been brought forward since its arrival in England.

In October a large number of the men were sent up to see the Great Exhibition of 1862 by the officers.

1863. The 83rd remained quartered at Dover until the 23rd April, when it marched to the camp at Shorncliffe, where it relieved the 69th Regiment, which had been sent to the Cape, and was quartered in C lines.

In May the regiment was inspected by Brigadier-General Sutton, Lieutenant-Colonel Hankey commanding.

PART VII

SERVICES OF THE REGIMENT, 1864-1907

LIEUTENANT COLTHURST was promoted vice Baumgartner transferred to Bombay Staff Corps, and Lieutenant Blunt appointed adjutant vice Colthurst.

1864. In April the regiment under Lieutenant-Colonel Hankey moved to Aldershot, and was quartered in the North Camp.

1865. The depôt of the regiment joined the regiment from Chatham, making the strength up to twelve companies.

In April the head-quarters, seven companies, moved to Sheffield, and the remaining five companies to Weedon.

In May two companies were sent to Bradford, in June one company to York; the latter returned to head-quarters in September, and the former in October.

In June and July detachments of the regiment were called upon to aid the civil power during riots in connection with the elections at Nottingham, Grantham, Lincoln, and Rotherham.

In October two companies were detached for duty at Tynemouth.

1866. In January the regiment embarked at Liverpool for Dublin, and was consequently distributed as under:—

Head-quarters . . .	Curragh.
Three companies . . .	Armagh.
One company . . .	Monaghan.
Two companies . . .	Sligo.
Two ,, . . .	Boyle.

In May the establishment was reduced to ten companies. Various changes in the stations of the detachments took place during the year, but at the end of the year the whole regiment moved to Richmond Barracks, Dublin.

On 27th December the regiment was armed with breech-loading converted Enfield rifles, Snider pattern.

1867. The depôt companies moved in March to Colchester, and in April the regiment embarked at Kingstown, and was conveyed by the troopship *Himalaya* to Gibraltar, where it relieved the 86th Regiment in the Casemate Barracks.

Lieutenant Tollemache died during April of this year.

On 9th May the regiment received the new colours, the presentation being made by the Hon. Lady Airey.

1868. Lieutenant Cooke Collis was appointed adjutant vice Blunt promoted.

1869. Captain Luke O'Connor died at Glasgow.

1870. On 11th March the regiment, under Colonel A. B. Hankey, embarked on the troopship *Tamar* and proceeded to Alexandria, marched to Suez, and embarked on the troopship *Euphrates* on 25th March. Arriving at Bombay on the 8th April, the regiment proceeded to Poona and was quartered in Wanourie Barracks.

In April, Ensign W. De Hoghton died at St. Remo.

In June the establishment was altered to eight companies.

1871. Captain R. H. James died at Poona in April.

In November three companies proceeded on detachment to Bombay, two to Sattara, and one to Asserghur.

On the 19th November, Colonel A. B. Hankey retired on half-pay, and was succeeded by Lieutenant-Colonel J. S. Brown.

1872. On the 11th November the whole regiment was assembled at Bombay, to provide guards of honour to Lord Northbrooke, the Viceroy, and for a viceregal durbar to invest the Begum of Bhopal with the "Star of India," and proceeded on detachment again on completion of these duties.

The depôt companies, which had apparently now left Colchester, and were stationed at Chatham, moved to Newry.

1873. The whole regiment was assembled at Chinchivad to take part in manœuvres, after which it left in December by rail to Ahmedabad, and leaving one company on detachment there, marched to Deesa,

1874. arriving there on 15th January. Companies were sent for change of air to Mount Aboo.

The "Glengarry" cap was taken into wear on 14th December, in place of one of the "Kilmarnock" pattern.

1875. Lieutenant G. Cleaveland died at Mount Aboo.
The depôt companies moved to Fermoy, and were attached to the 86th Regiment.

Lieutenant G. Beresford shot himself at Deesa.

Two companies proceeded to Baroda on detachment in October, at which place the regiment found guards of honour on the 18th and 23rd November for the arrival and departure of H.R.H. the Prince of Wales.

1876. Lieutenant A. H. Oakeley died at Deesa on 10th October.

In December one company from Deesa and the three composing the detachments at Ahmedabad and Baroda marched to Porebundur and embarked on the I.G.S. *Dalhousie* for Karachi; and then with the 50th Regiment were sent, on account of smallpox, into camp at Jemadar Ha Laudi.

The head-quarters of the regiment marched from

Deesa to Mandavi, and arriving at this place (twenty-three marches) on 10th January, 1877, proceeded on the *Dalhousie* to Karachi, where they were joined by the companies from camp.

1877.

In February two companies were sent on detachment to Hyderabad.

The depôt companies, now at the Curragh, moved to Aldershot.

1878. On 11th November telegraphic instructions were received at Karachi for the regiment to be in readiness for field-service in Upper Sind.

On 12th December, invalids, women, and children were sent, under Lieutenant Bell, viâ Bombay to Ahmednagar, and on 21st December the head-quarters (five companies), under Colonel T. S. Brown, proceeded on service to Sukkur, where on 5th January, 1879, they were joined by the three companies from Hyderabad, and on 30th January by a detachment from home. Of this draft 83 men came from the linked battalion (86th Foot).

1879.

The strength at Sukkur was then—20 officers, 41 sergeants, 15 drummers, and 779 men.

The regiment was encamped about 1½ miles south of Sukkur on the bank of the Indus.

The regiment left Sukkur, by detachments, between 20th February and 5th March, and returned by rail to Karachi, and was encamped on the Maidan.

On 13th March the regiment, under Colonel Brown, embarked on the I.G.S.'s *Tenasserim* and *Czarewitch*, and proceeded to Vingorla, where the party from Ahmednagar joined it, and marched by easy marches to Belgaum. One company was quartered in the fort and the remainder in barracks.

On 29th September, Colonel Brown was appointed to the Brigade Staff to command Sind District, and was succeeded in the command by Lieutenant-Colonel E. Meurant.

1880. In February, two companies were sent on detachment to Sattara.

In September, as the regiment was about to proceed to England, volunteers to the number of 82 rank and file were transferred to other corps.

The detachment from Sattara returned to headquarters in December.

Instructions had been received in November that the regiment would proceed to England in H.M.S. *Jumna* on 25th January, 1881, but on 3rd January of

1881. that year, a telegram was received ordering the regiment to Natal on field service owing to the outbreak of hostilities with the Boers.

The regiment left Belgaum on 7th January, marched to Vingorla, and on the 15th embarked on H.M.S. *Crocodile* (on which were also the Gordon Highlanders) for Durban; 46 invalids with the women and children proceeded to Bombay *en route* to England.

On 30th January the regiment, consisting of 20 officers, 574 rank and file, landed at Durban, and proceeded by rail to standing camp at Fillie Fontein; there it only remained for two weeks and then marched to Pietermaritzburg, thence to the base of operations, Newcastle, where it arrived on 9th March—a march rendered extremely difficult owing to heavy rains.

During March, April, and May the regiment was variously encamped at Signal Hill, Bennett's Drift, and elsewhere, and employed wood-cutting, coal-mining, etc.

On 1st July, the following changes took effect (General Order No. 41 of 1881):—

The regiment (83rd Foot) became the 1st Battalion Royal Irish Rifles.

The regiment (86th Foot) became the 2nd Battalion Royal Irish Rifles.

The Royal North Down Militia became the 3rd Battalion Royal Irish Rifles.

The Antrim Militia became the 4th Battalion Royal Irish Rifles.

The Royal South Down Militia became the 5th Battalion Royal Irish Rifles.

And by General Order No. 70 of 1881:—

The Louth Militia became the 6th Battalion Royal Irish Rifles.

The No. 83 was assigned to the Regimental District.

The uniform was changed to "green with light green facings," and the following badges and devices were added:—

"The Sphinx," "The Harp and Crown."

Motto—"Quis Separabit."

Distinctions—"Egypt," "India," "Bourbon."

In November, hostilities came to an end, and the force about Newcastle was broken up.

The regiment marched from Bennett's Drift on 7th November, arrived at Pietermaritzburg on the 19th, and proceeded by train to Durban, arriving on 21st November.

On 23rd November it embarked on H.M.S. *Tamar* for England.

1882. On 3rd January the *Tamar* arrived at Portsmouth. The regiment disembarked next day and proceeded by rail to Dover, consisting of 15 officers and 489 rank and file.

On 14th March, H.R.H. the Duke of Cambridge inspected the regiment.

On 29th June, rifle uniform was taken into wear.

In August, owing to war in Egypt, the First Class Reserve was called up, but demobilized again in October.

In September permission was received (General Order No. 252 of 1882) for the regiment to "bear Cape of Good Hope 1806," instead of "Cape of Good Hope" on their appointments.

1883. The battalion remained at Dover.

1884. A detachment, under Captain H. H. Jackson, proceeded to Halifax, N.S., to join the 2nd Battalion.

On 13th August, the battalion, under Colonel Meurant, proceeded in H.M.S. *Assistance* to Guernsey, sending four companies to Alderney.

On 5th October, Colonel Meurant was placed on half-pay, and was succeeded in the command by Lieutenant-Colonel F. Karslake.

1885. A draft, under Lieutenants Welman and O'Leary, proceeded to Halifax, N.S., to join the 2nd Battalion.

On 15th December, the battalion moved from Guernsey and Alderney to Gosport.

1886. The battalion remained at Gosport.

1887. In February, Colonel Karslake was succeeded by Colonel C. J. Burnett from the East Yorkshire Regiment.

On 7th July, the battalion proceeded to Aldershot to take part on 9th July in the Jubilee Review, held on the completion of the fiftieth year of reign of H.M. Queen Victoria. Strength present—19 officers and 617 rank and file, and was brigaded with 2nd Battalion Rifle Brigade and 2nd Battalion King's Royal Rifles.

The battalion returned to Gosport on 12th July.

On 14th December, the battalion moved to Ireland and was stationed at Mullingar, with a detachment at Sligo.

1888-9. The battalion remained at Mullingar.

1890. Colonel Burnett having been appointed A.A. General at Aldershot, Lieutenant-Colonel H. D. Cutbill, from half-pay, succeeded to the command.

In July, the battalion moved to the Curragh for drills, and in August to "New Barracks," Fermoy, with a detachment of one company at Fort Carlisle, Queenstown.

1891. A rifle busby was sanctioned and taken into wear on Christmas Day.

1892. Captain Curzon was appointed adjutant vice Wilkinson.

1893. The battalion moved from Fermoy to Newry on 19th June, sending a detachment in October to Drogheda.

1894. A field-service cap was taken into use in place of the Glengarry, which had been worn since 1874.

On 4th June, Major R. J. Knox was promoted lieutenant-colonel, and succeeded to the command vice Cutbill, whose four years of command had terminated.

On 16th October, the battalion moved to Brighton. Strength—20 officers and 784 rank and file, sending two companies as a detachment to Chichester.

1895. The regiment was armed with Lee-Enfield rifles, Mark II.

1896. Lieutenant O. C. Baker was appointed adjutant on 1st January, vice Captain Curzon, whose tenure expired.

On 27th April, Lieutenant King-Harman with 1 colour-sergeant, 1 sergeant, and 25 men, proceeded to South Africa as part of an Irish company of mounted infantry for service in Matabeleland.

On 21st September, the battalion, numbering 16 officers, 586 rank and file, moved by rail to Aldershot, and was quartered in Ramillies' Barracks.

On 3rd November, Lieutenant-Colonel C. Haggard

succeeded to the command vice Lieutenant-Colonel R. J. Knox.

1897. On 9th January, Lieutenant-General H.R.H. the Duke of Connaught commanding Aldershot District inspected the battalion. Captain O'Leary received and was permitted to wear the 4th Class Order of the Osmanieh, for services in the Dongola expedition.

On 24th April, the battalion embarked at Southampton on the transport *Dunera* for South Africa, and having disembarked at Durban on 24th May—strength 20 officers, 593 rank and file, 37 women, and 51 children—proceeded by rail to Ladysmith.

On 25th May the detachment under Lieutenant King-Harman rejoined head-quarters. This detachment had been employed on service for thirteen months with head-quarters at Fort Salisbury, and had had 1 man wounded. It received the thanks of the G.O.C. Natal and Zululand for "their soldierly qualities and good behaviour," and subsequently received a medal for service in Rhodesia.

On 27th September, the battalion was put into khaki clothing.

1898. On 10th August, a Maxim machine gun was issued to the battalion.

1899. On 24th March, the battalion left Ladysmith for Durban, where it embarked on R.I.M.S. *Clive* for Calcutta, and arriving on 15th April, it proceeded to Dum Dum.

On 18th September, the head-quarters moved to Fort William, Calcutta.

War with the Boers in South Africa having broken out, Captain Fox-Strangways and Lieutenant Eckford were sent there for service on 18th September, and on 20th September, 1 sergeant and 14 men also went as trained transport drivers.

1900. On 1st January, Lieutenant Macnamara succeeded to the adjutancy vice Baker, whose tenure expired.

On 1st February, Captain Noblett and 1 sergeant were attached to Lumsden's Horse, a volunteer Mounted Infantry Corps, and proceeded to South Africa.

On 28th October, Lieutenant-Colonel A. T. Swaine succeeded to the command vice Haggard.

On 18th December, Lieutenant G. Forbes died from enteric fever.

1901. Captain Noblett and 1 sergeant returned to duty from South Africa. This officer was mentioned in despatches.

The battalion remained at Calcutta.

1902. On 3rd February, the battalion moved to Fyzabad.

On 14th February, 4 sergeants, 6 corporals, and 139 privates left from Bombay to join the 2nd Battalion on service in South Africa.

On 10th March, Lieutenant Low was killed in action in South Africa.

On 14th March, Major F. J. Tobin, who had joined as second-in-command, was decorated on parade with the Distinguished Service Order for service in South Africa.

On 18th November, the battalion went to Delhi and took part in the great Durbar held for the proclamation of H.M. King Edward VII as Emperor of India, and the following officers, warrant officers, N.C.O.'s, and riflemen received the coronation medal given for this occasion :—

Lieut.-Col. Swaine.
Major Tobin, D.S.O.
Lieut. Dunn.
Sgt.-Major Foster.
Bd.-Major Williams.

Colour Sergt. Cowden.
Colour Sergt. Elphick.
Corporal Verdon.
Rifleman Heron.

Subsequently it took part in manœuvres near Delhi, and returned to Fyzabad on 21st January, 1903.

1903. On 20th August, Sergeant Bingham went on service to Somaliland.

Sergeant-Major Foster was promoted Quartermaster on 9th November.

1904. On 1st January, Captain H. R. Charley succeeded Captain Macnamara as adjutant.

On 20th May, a machine-gun detachment of 1 sergeant and 6 men under Lieutenant Bowen-Colthurst proceeded to Thibet with the mission under Brigadier-General (afterwards Sir) R. Macdonald, C.B., and subsequently received a medal for this service.

On 28th October, Colonel Swaine completed his tenure of command and was succeeded by Lieutenant-Colonel J. S. Brown.

On 15th December the battalion left Fyzabad and marched to Meerut, 351 miles, arriving on 1st January.

1905. *En route* two companies were detached for duty at Delhi.

On 30th November the battalion left by train for Rawal Pindi and took part in manœuvres and review on the occasion of the visit of T.R.H.'s the Prince and Princess of Wales.

During 1905–7 the battalion remained at Meerut, having a detachment at Delhi, and (during the hot seasons) at Chakrata and Landour.

1906. Lieutenant Robinson died at Meerut.

In January the battalion went to Agra and took part in a review held in honour of a visit to India of H.M. the Ameer of Afghanistan.

1907. On 6th March, Captain Charley's tenure of the adjutancy expired and Lieutenant H. R. Goodman was appointed.

The following is a LIST *of all* OFFICERS KILLED *and* WOUNDED *in the Regiment since it was raised in* 1793.

KILLED.

Colonel William Fitch	Maroon War.
Lieutenant-Colonel Gordon	Talavera.
,, Collins	Salamanca.
Major Widrington	Vittoria.
Brevet Major Hon. Powys	Talavera.
Captain Lee	Maroon War.
,, Fry	Badajos.
,, Samuel Read	Jeerun, India.
Lieutenant Montgomery	Talavera.
,, Dahman	Do.
,, Flood	Do.
,, Ferris	Fuentes d'Onor.
,, Lindsay	Vittoria.
,, Bloxham	Do.
,, Johnson	Canada.
,, Low	South Africa.
Ensign Hackett	Peninsula.

WOUNDED.

Lieutenant-Colonel Collins	Albuera.
,, Carr	Orthes.
Major Blaquiere	Do.
Captain Venables	Vittoria.
,, Brunt	Maroon War.
,, Summerfield	Talavera.
,, Reynolds	Do.
,, Elliott	Orthes.
,, Venables	Do.
Lieutenant Abel	Talavera.
,, Johnstone	Do.
,, Nicholson	Do.
,, Pine	Do.
,, Boggie	Do.
,, Baldwin	Do.
,, Ferris	Do.
,, Colthurst	Busaco.
,, Vereker	Fuentes d'Onor.
,, Matthews	Ciudad Rodrigo.
,, Vereker	Do.
,, Broomfield	Badajos.

MEMOIRS OF THE 83RD REGIMENT

WOUNDED.

Lieutenant O'Neill	. . .	Badajos.
,, Bowles	. . .	Do.
,, Lane	. . .	Do.
,, Vavasour	. . .	Do.
,, Baldwin	. . .	Do.
,, Gascoigne	. . .	Salamanca.
,, Smith	. . .	Vittoria.
,, Baldwin	. . .	Do.
,, Barry	. . .	Do.
,, Watson	. . .	Nivelle.
,, Barry	. . .	Do.
,, Wyatt	. . .	Do.
,, Baldwin	. . .	Orthes.
,, Watson	. . .	Do.
,, Lane	. . .	Do.
,, Hingstone	. . .	Vic Bigorre.
,, Lane	. . .	Do.
Lieut. and Adj. Swinburne	.	Orthes.
Adjutant Brahan	. .	Talavera.
Lieut. and Adj. J. Swinburne	.	Do.
Ensign Nugent	. . .	Orthes.
,, Burgess	. . .	Nivelle.
,, A. Tulloch	. . .	Talavera.
,, Barry	. . .	Do.
,, Carey	. . .	Do.
,, Irwin	. . .	Do.
Assistant-Surgeon Miles	.	Nimbharia.

TOTAL.

	Killed.	Wounded.
Lieutenant-Colonels	3	2
Majors	2	1
Captains	3	6
Lieutenants	7	31
Ensigns	1	7
Surgeons	0	1
	16	48

GRAND TOTAL.

	Killed.	Wounded.
Officers	16	48
Sergeants and rank and file	279	810
	295	858

LIST OF OFFICERS *who have served in the 83rd Regiment, compiled from the " Officers' Records," preserved in the Regimental Orderly Room.*

COLONELS COMMANDING.	REMARKS.
William Fitch	1793 : Colonel Commandant.
James Balfour	1795 : Major-General.
John Hodgson	1823 : Major-General.
Hastings Fraser, C.B.	1835 : Major-General.
Sir Fred. Stovin, G.C.B., K.C.M.G.	1848 : Lieutenant-General.
E. P. Buckley	1865 : General. Died 29th May, 1873.
W. G. Brown	1873 : General. Died 27th Nov., 1883.
W. H. Bradford	Lieutenant-General.

COLONELS OR LIEUTENANT-COLONELS COMMANDING.

William Fitch	Killed in the Maroon War.
William Sleigh	
Thomas Gibson	
Sir Edward Baynes	
William Godley	
John Byne Skerritt	
Joseph Baird	
William Hutchinson	
Alexander Gordon	Killed at Talavera.
Richard Collins	Killed at Salamanca.
Jacob Blunt	
John Potter Hamilton	
Sir Henry William Carr	
Charles Cother	Retired, 1829.
—— Bunbury	
Hon. H. Dundas, C.B.	Retired on half-pay, 1842.
B. Trydell	Brevet Colonel, promoted to Major-General, 1856.
W. H. Law	Retired on full pay, as Major-General, 1856.
J. Kelsall	Retired on full pay, as Colonel, 1858.
Edward Steele, C.B.	Retired July, 1862. Died in London, 6th August, 1862.
Charles W. Austen	Exchanged to 14th Regiment.

88

MEMOIRS OF THE 83RD REGIMENT

Colonels or Lieutenant-Colonels Commanding.	Remarks.
A. Barnard Hankey	Retired 2nd August, 1871.
T. S. Brown	To Brigade Staff 28th February, 1880.
E. Meurant	Retired 5th October, 1884.
F. Karslake	Retired 12th February, 1887.
C. J. Burnett	To Staff 4th June, 1890.
H. D. Cutbill	Retired 4th June, 1894.
R. J. Knox	Retired 28th October, 1896.
C. Haggard	Retired 28th October, 1900.
A. T. Swaine	Retired 28th October, 1904.
J. S. Brown	Now commanding.

Lieutenant-Colonels.

S. Flower	Retired 5th October, 1888.
C. G. Gore	Retired 10th January, 1883.
R. O. De Montmorency	To 2 R.I.R. 10th January, 1883.

Majors.

T. Summerfield	Died at Limerick, 1834.
Peter Crofton	Retired.
Joseph Swinburne	Brevet Lieutenant-Colonel, retired as Colonel, 1853. Died, 1860.
Edward Townsend	Died of cholera at Kurrachee, 1851.
Henry F. Ainslie	Retired as Lieut.-Col. on full pay, 1855.
Henry Lloyd	Died of cholera at Cambay, 1854.
John Heatley	Brevet Lieutenant-Colonel; exchanged to 69th Regiment.
James F. Murray	Exchanged to 97th Regiment, 1862.
Edward B. Cooke	Retired, 1862.
Henry De R. Pigott	Exchanged to 19th Regiment, 1863.
Thomas Venables	
Robert Bates	
J. S. Wakefield	Brevet Lieutenant-Colonel; retired 7th August, 1878.
F. A. Wright	Retired 18th January, 1882.
E. A. Butler	Retired 18th April, 1885.
J. P. B. Forster	Retired 16th September, 1868.
G. G. Beazley	Retired 12th March, 1881.
C. J. Wyndham	Transferred to 2 R.I.R. 18th Sept., 1888.
B. H. Metcalfe	Retired 31st December, 1887.
H. H. Stuart	To 2 R.I.R., 1889.
W. Cooke Collis	Promoted half-pay Lieutenant-Colonel, and retired 4th May, 1892.
F. S. F. Stokes	Transferred to 2 R.I.R., 1st August, 1890.
J. J. Meynell	Retired 2nd March, 1893.
H. A. Eager	Transferred to 2 R.I.R., December, 1895.
W. Ayde	To Staff, 25th March, 1898.

MAJORS.

E. Allen	Exchanged to 2 R.I.R , 29th April, 1899.
F. J. Tobin	Promoted into 2 R.I.R., 28th July, 1904.
W. J. McWhinnie	Retired 21st September, 1906.
F. E. P. Curzon	Appointed second in command 2 R.I.R., 13th July, 1905.
W. E. O'Leary	
H. M. Cliff	Retired 17th October, 1902.
K. Beresford	
F. J. H. Bell	
C. E. R. Harvey	
G. B. Laurie	Exchanged to 2 R.I.R.
A. V. Weir	
O. C. Baker	

CAPTAINS.

Henry Caulfield	Removed to 58th Foot, 1833.
Francis Johnston	Retired, 1834.
Aretas S. Young	Exchanged to 63rd Regiment, 1835.
John Richardson	Retired, 1840.
Robert Colquohoun	Died in London, 1841.
John Harrison	Half-pay, 1839.
Robert Kelly	Sold out, 1839.
J. H. Anstruther	Sold out, 1839.
George Grey	Sold out, 1840.
John Rayson	Sold out, 1841.
Denis McC. Stubbeman	Sold out, 1845.
John Emslie	Sold out, 1844.
Edward D'Alton	Half-pay.
Thomas St. Aubyn	Died at Putney, 1846.
Benjamin H. Brown	Retired, 1847.
Duncan Campbell	Exchanged to 90th Regiment, 1848.
William Garston	Half-pay, 1849.
D. R. De Rinzy	Half-pay, 1849; died of cholera same year.
Hon. William Gage	Died at Poona, 1849.
D. W. P. Labalmondiere	Half-pay, 1850.
S. H. F. Cary	Exchanged to 31st Regiment, 1850.
David Anderson	Exchanged to 22nd Regiment.
Frederick Woodgate	Retired, 1848.
Thomas Spring	Exchanged to 35th Regiment, 1851.
Samuel B. Lamb	Exchanged to 10th Regiment, 1851.
Thomas Adams	Exchanged to 78th Regiment, 1854.
Frederick George Moore	Half-pay, 1855.
Thomas M. Keogh	Retired, 1856.
William Mills Molony	Exchanged to 22nd Regiment.
Samuel Read	Killed in action at Jeerun, 1857.
Robert Colville Jones	Died at Ahmedabad, 1857.

MEMOIRS OF THE 83RD REGIMENT

CAPTAINS.	REMARKS.
William Nott	Died near Birmingham, 1858.
Herbert Stanley Cooper	Died at Nusseerabad, 1858.
Hon. E. G. W. Forester	Half-pay, 1858.
Robert H. P. Crawford	Exchanged to 90th Regiment ; died in Crimea.
John Sharman Molony	Removed to Staff—Falkland Islands.
Richard R. Wyvill	Retired, 1860.
Thomas Parker Wright	Staff officer of pensioners.
F. H. D. Marsh	Exchanged to 89th Regiment.
Henry Gandy	Retired, 1860.
Retired J. Sweeney	Half-pay.
T. Mowbray Baumgartner	Transferred to Bombay Staff Corps, 1861.
James Verling Ellis	Exchanged to Ceylon Rifles, 1862.
William Minhear	Retired, 1863.
F. Pemberton Campbell	Exchanged to 14th Hussars, 1863.
Frederick Dickenson	Retired, 1863.
Edward William Bray	Brevet major.
John Sprot	
Edward Meurant	
Julian Wakefield	
Chas. C. Gore	
James F. Sweeney	
Geo. G. Beazley	
Geo. L. Huyshe	
William H. Ivimy	
Lawrence Mackenzie	
G. F. Stehelin	Retired 6th November, 1868.
J. K. S. Henderson	Retired 9th April, 1890.
L. E. O'Connor	Died 10th January, 1869.
G. P. Fawkes	Retired 29th June, 1870.
P. C. Browne	Exchanged to 23rd Foot 2nd May, 1869.
J. F. Wyse	
W. C. Strickland	Retired 28th October, 1871.
C. L. Smith	Retired 30th April, 1873.
G. E. E. Blunt	Retired 5th January, 1870.
F. H. A. D. Roebuck	Exchanged to 46th Foot 20th July, 1870.
E. G. Johnson	Retired 28th May, 1870.
R. H. James	Died at Poona 4th April, 1871.
G. N. Stevenson	Exchanged to 91st Foot 31st Oct., 1871.
G. W. Cockburn	Retired 30th September, 1870.
G. E. S. Cartwright	Retired 10th February, 1877.
C. J. Shorburn	Retired 5th November, 1884.
W. Stewart	Retired 9th June, 1877.
T. F. Gibbs	Retired 19th October, 1878.
H. C. Bond	Died 27th March, 1882.
C. T. Davenport	To Army Pay Dept. 26th August, 1881.

MEMOIRS OF THE 83RD REGIMENT

Captains.	Remarks.
J. A. R. Bell	To Army Pay Dept. 12th April, 1881.
J. W. H. Anson	Superseded 19th July, 1882.
W. B. Marling	Resigned 16th January, 1884.
E. C. L. Walter	Died at Alderney 4th May, 1885.
R. Taylor	Retired 11th July, 1884.
R. S. Graves	To Army Pay Dept. 9th December, 1885.
Hon. F. L. Colborne	Brevet Major to Staff, April, 1885.
M. E. Mulchinock	Resigned 17th August, 1887.
C. G. Harris	Retired 10th August, 1888.
L. T. V. Wilkinson	Retired 20th February, 1895.
A. W. Raymond	To 2 R.I.R. 1st February, 1888.
W. H. Dunlop	To 2 R.I.R. 20th May, 1892.
H. L. Welman	To Militia, Adjutant 20th Nov., 1893.
G. O. Callaghan Westrapp	Retired 20th February, 1889.
J. E. Hodges	To Army Pay Department 1st July, 1893.
W. G. Lillingston	To half-pay 12th July, 1896.
R. A. D. Rowley	Died 19th November, 1898.
G. W. W. D'Arcy Evans	To 20th Hussars 10th June, 1895.
P. M. H. Carew	Retired 3rd July, 1897.
T. S. Fox Strangways	To Staff 22nd October, 1899 (retired).
A. F. Ryan	Resigned 24th August, 1898.
H. F. R. Despard	Retired 15th August, 1902.
W. E. O. C. Blunt	To Army Pay Department 29th April, 1908.
T. Carson	To Adjutant 5 R.I.R. 22nd February, 1900 (retired).
A. J. B. Addison	To Adjutant, Artists' Vols. (retired).
B. H. M. Fox	To A.S.C. 15th October, 1900.
P. G. W. Eckford	Adjutant, Vols. 14th November, 1905.
H. G. Breman	To half-pay 8th May, 1902 (retired).
D. W. Silwell	Brevet Major. Exchanged to 2 R.I.R. 10th October, 1903.
L. H. Noblett	Brevet Major. Promoted to 2 R.I.R., 1907.
H. R. Charley	To 2 R.I.R. 6th March, 1907.
L. C. Sprague	To 2 R.I.R.
C. C. Macnamara	
J. H. Alston	
B. Allgood	
E. G. Dunn	
E. H. Saunders, D.S.O.	To Sr. T. Corps 24th November, 1905.
R. H. S. Dashwood	Retired 21st December, 1907.
C. H. Dixon	To 2 R.I.R.
L. G. B. Rodney	
E. C. Monro	
J. C. Bowen-Colthurst	

MEMOIRS OF THE 83RD REGIMENT

LIEUTENANTS.	REMARKS.
Edward De Visme	Retired, 1831.
Henry S. G. Bowles	Died at Ballinrobe, 1832.
George Blakeney	Retired, 1835.
John J. E. Hamilton	Retired, 1833.
W. S. Johnson	Killed in action at Prescott, 1838.
Hanway Howard	Retired, 1837.
W. S. Ducie	Retired, 1838.
C. T. Egerton	Retired, 1839.
Roger Coghlan	Died in Dublin, 1834.
William J. Nunn	Half-pay.
James Goodrich	Retired, 1839.
Hon. R. H. Clifford	Killed from his horse at Limerick, 1833.
T. Taubman James	Retired.
Francis W. Bowles	Exchanged to 94th, 1837.
Wenman Wynniatt	Drowned at London, Canada, 1841.
James Clerk	Exchanged to 9th Light Dragoons.
James Foster	Exchanged to 1st Dragoon Guards.
William Blackburne	To 91st Regiment.
Thomas Stewart Lane	Died at Castlecomer, 1848.
Walter Hamilton	Retired, 1845.
Francis J. Hext	Retired, 1845.
John W. Crowe	Retired 1849
John William Wallington	Exchanged to 4th Light Dragoons, 1847.
Sir Richard Gethin, Bart.	Retired, 1846.
James Sadler Naylor	Exchanged to 8th Hussars, 1846.
John T. Downman	Retired, 1849.
W. Sandford Wills	Exchanged to 5th Dragoon Guards.
Lord Alfred S. Churchill	Retired, 1848.
H. P. Villiers Villiers	Retired, 1855.
W. C. Sheills	Retired, 1852.
Chas. Peregrine Teesdale	Promoted to 55th Regiment, 1855.
S. W. F. M. Wilson	Do.
John Meade	Promoted to 30th Regiment, 1856.
John Norris McKelvey	Died at Deesa, 1856.
Braithwaite Chamley	Exchanged to 17th Lancers, 1858.
Thomas Rowland	Exchanged to 1st Regiment, 1853.
Usher W. Alcock	Retired, 1855.
Marmaduke N. Richardson	Retired, 1853.
William Fitzroy	Promoted into 63rd Regiment, 1855.
John W. Huskisson	Transferred to 56th Regiment, 1855.
Stephen W. Metge	Died at sea, 1856.
J. R. A. Colebrook	Died at Mysana, 1860.
G. W. H. Wardell	Retired, 1861.
Guildford M. Onslow	Retired, 1861.
John Healey	Exchanged to 66th Regiment, 1862.
Edwin Thomas	Retired, 1862.

Lieutenants.	Remarks.
R. Kenneth Gibb	Exchanged to 1st West India Regiment, 1863.
H. G. Davies	Exchanged to 96th Regiment, 1863.
James E. Brymer	Drowned at Hythe, 1863.
William K. Bookey	Retired, 1853.
George Dunlevie	Half-pay, 1857.
Alfred Holt	Promoted into 21st Regiment, 1855.
Thomas G. Coote	
Peter C. Browne	
Nicholas Pennefather	
Frederick Karslake	
W. Forbes Anderson	Died at Sandgate, 1863.
Hubert C. Whitlock	
Michael Murphy	
Littleton A. Powys	
James Geo. Scott	
Henry Albert Fuller	
Walter C. Strickland	
Frederick Augustus Wright	
Charles Lucius Smith	
Charles Hay Tollemache	
John Olphert Gage	
Thos. E. B. Townsend	
C. Horrocks	Retired 7th November, 1868.
H. L. Parry	Retired 1st February, 1873.
T. P. Powell	Retired 26th July, 1873.
H. W. Walker	Transferred to 2nd 19th Foot.
H. V. H. Brooke	Exchanged to 33rd Foot 1st December, 1869.
M. O. Kirkward	Retired 16th March, 1861.
W. F. Marriott	Exchanged to 41st Foot, 1875.
A. Fawcett	Retired 8th July, 1868.
J. W. Anderson	To Bombay Staff Corps, 11th July, 1874.
E. Bruce	Transferred to 39th Foot.
A. Chichester	Exchanged to 95th Foot, 31st August, 1870.
W. De Hogton	Died at S. Remo, 29th April, 1870.
R. W. S. Burnett	Retired 10th July, 1872.
Hon. E. F. Gifford	Exchanged to 2nd 24th Foot, 25th February, 1873.
C. W. Hinde	To Bombay Staff Corps, 7th February, 1873.
J. H. Hardtman Berckley	Transferred to 107th Regiment, 15th January, 1875.
L. F. Heath	To Indian Staff Corps, 1871.
C. G. B. Hervey	To Indian Staff Corps, 1878.
G. Cleaveland	Died at Mount Aboo, 19th March, 1895.

MEMOIRS OF THE 83RD REGIMENT

LIEUTENANTS.	REMARKS.
G. A. Beresford	Died at Deesa, 8th June, 1875.
P. A. Buckland	To Bengal Staff Corps, 24th April, 1875.
H. F. Cadell	To Madras Staff Corps, 25th November, 1876.
C. St. L. Wilkinson	Retired 25th November, 1874.
A. C. G. Mayne	To I.S.C., 1st September, 1877.
J. W. Hogge	To I.S.C., 23rd May, 1876.
C. H. W. Alexander	Resigned 30th October, 1878.
H. E. W. Beville	To I.S.C., 14th December, 1875.
A. W. Ancketill	Resigned 7th June, 1875.
H. Read	To Bengal Staff Corps.
H. B. Warden	To Bombay Staff Corps, 1876.
J. M. Johnstone	Retired 26th November, 1879.
A. D. Enriquerz	To I.S.C., 29th November, 1881.
H. Mansfield	To I.S.C., 5th August, 1878.
G. F. N. Ginley	To Bombay Staff Corps.
D. Cole	To I.S.C., 19th July, 1878.
L. B. H. Baker	To I.S.C.
W. D. Thomson	To I.S.C., 29th August, 1882.
G. R. D. Westrapp	To I.S.C., 26th April, 1880.
J. F. Trant	Exchanged to 2nd West India Regiment, 2nd August, 1882.
G. V. Burrows	To I.S.C.
R. W. F. Monteith	To A.S.C., 18th April, 1885.
A. P. S. Barnett	To I.S.C., 16th March, 1882.
E. A. Kettlewell	To I.S.C., 18th December, 1880.
W. G. Alban	To I.S.R., 9th November, 1880.
W. Browne	
M. A. Tighe	
H. F. Battersby	Retired 29th October, 1883.
J. Fisher	To 2nd Norfolk Regt., 7th Nov., 1883.
C. H. Orpen	Resigned 29th June, 1887.
J. R. Gray	To K.R. Rifles, 18th January, 1886.
H. R. Homfray	Transferred to 1st Life Guards, 7th November, 1888.
J. F. Stewart	Transferred to S. Rifles, 14th April, 1883.
G. W. Palin	Transferred to North Stafford Regiment, 12th June, 1883.
A. W. Hasted	Transferred to 2nd Wilts Regiment, 25th August, 1885.
J. H. Lowry	To I.S.C., 5th May, 1887.
F. F. Bradshaw	To I.S.C., 2nd March, 1887.
G. W. Massey	Promoted into 2nd Battalion, 2nd March, 1893.
A. P. M. Burke	Resigned 2nd March, 1903.
E. W. H. Somerset	To Rifle Brigade, 3rd August, 1887.
A. H. Festing	To Royal Niger Coy., 29th July, 1885.

MEMOIRS OF THE 83RD REGIMENT

LIEUTENANTS.	REMARKS.
G. S. Carey	Transferred to 2nd R.I. Rifles, 23rd July, 1895. Died at Poona.
M. S. D. Westrapp	Resigned 8th June, 1898.
H. L. Low	Killed on service with 2nd R.I. Rifles in South Africa, 10th May, 1902.
W. A. King Harmen	
H. Wilding	Resigned 14th September, 1898.
R. L. Hughes Hallett	To Indian Army, 3rd October, 1900.
A. G. Forbes	Died at Dum Dum, 18th December, 1900.
C. S. Dixon	Promoted into 2nd R.I. Rifles.
C. L. W. Wallace	Resigned 13th June, 1905.
A. S. Kirkwood	To S. and T. Corps, 1st November, 1906.
W. M. Lanyon	
A. J. Biscoe	
H. R. Goodman	
W. M. Culloch	Resigned, 1907.
F. Robinson	Died at Meerut, 11th April, 1906.
Hon. B. A. Forbes	
E. M. A. J. Hogan	
G. A. Chatterton	
P. F. J. Smith	
J. F. Martyr	
C. C. Tee	
Geo. H. Cazalet	Promoted to 18th Regiment.
Robert Portal	Promoted to 41st Regiment.
T. G. L. Carew Gwyn	Exchanged to 6th Dragoon Guards, 1847.
W. T. Riley	To 52nd Regiment.
William A. Riddell	Retired.
H. M. Scott	Died at Manchester, 1832.
Frederick Ford	Retired, 1858.
James Pringle	Promoted.
Thomas Graham	Died at Kurrachee, 1852.
Graham Mylne	Promoted to 82nd Regiment.
William Blathway	Killed accidentally at Ilfracombe, 1859.
Geo. E. E. Blunt	
Henry Geo. Wilson	
A. Goring Bridger	
Henry Church	
James M. Lyall	
Sir Keith G. Jackson, Bart.	
R. O. De Montmorency	
John Blurton	
Anthony McClymont	Died at Deesa, 1856.
A. Crowley	Transferred to 48th Foot 1st May, 1878.
H. B. Brown	Transferred to 2 R.I.R. 27th May, 1888.
C. Gosling	Transferred to K.R.R. 28th Nov., 1888.

MEMOIRS OF THE 83RD REGIMENT

LIEUTENANTS.	REMARKS.
H. M. Biddulph	Transferred to Rifle Brigade, 6th February, 1889.
J. Murray	Died 25th October, 1898.
C. B. L. Clery	To I.S.C.
R. G. Baker	To I.C.S. 15th January, 1900.
R. C. Wilson	Resigned 1st October, 1901.
H. A. Gaussen	Resigned 7th April, 1906.
L. Pilkington	Resigned 1st November, 1901.
T. H. Barton	To Indian Army 16th November, 1903.
H. N. Jones	Exchanged to 2 R.I.R. 8th August, 1903.
A. H. Parsons	To Indian Army.
G. S. Scott	
E. C. Kenny	To Indian Army, 1903.
E. R. Ludlow Hewitt	
N. Hutcheson	
R. O. Mansergh	
E. De W. Waller	
A. W. Galway	

PAYMASTERS.	
Richard Brough	Retired, 1849.
John Denis Swinburne	
F. Fereday	Exchanged to 95th Foot, 31st Oct., 1871.
F. Scrivener	Transferred to A.P.D. 1st April, 1878.

ADJUTANTS.	
John Stubbs	Died at Kingston, 1840.
B. H. Browne	Promoted.
William Nott	Do.
William Hall	Died at Kurrachee, 1851.
Edward H. M. Mainwaring	Died at Poona, 1856.
James Nicholas Colthurst	
G. E. E. Blunt	
W. Coake Collis	27th June, 1871.
H. H. Berkeley	To 21st November, 1875.
F. S. F. Stokes	To 19th October, 1878.
W. B. Marling	To 16th December, 1882.
J. S. Brown	To 26th April, 1886.
F. J. H. Bell	To 25th May, 1890.
L. T. V. Wilkinson	To 1st January, 1892.
F. E. P. Curzon	To 31st December, 1895.
O. C. Baker	To 31st December, 1899.
C. C. Macnamara	To 31st December, 1903.
H. R. Charley	To 31st December, 1906.
H. R. Goodman	

MEMOIRS OF THE 83RD REGIMENT

QUARTERMASTERS.	REMARKS.
John Rusher	Retired, 1838.
Robert Imray	Retired, 1844.
Joseph Cartmail	Exchanged to 3rd Regiment, 1847.
William Colburn	Died at Poona, 1852.
Patrick Hayes	Retired as Captain, 1863.
T. Copeland	
M. McQuade	Transferred to 6 R.I.R., 7th January, 1882.
H. Jones	Transferred to 3 R.I.R., 10th June, 1882.
J. McGarty	Retired 23rd August, 1883.
L. Duffy	Superseded 24th October, 1884.
P. J. Thorpe	Cashiered 3rd November, 1893.
J. Cunningham	Died in South Africa, 1st March, 1898.
G. T. Drage	To Depôt, 21st October, 1903.
H. W. Foster	

SURGEONS.	
Samuel A. Piper, M.D.	Removed to 30th Regiment, 1830.
James Cross	Half-pay, 1837.
John Maitland	Exchanged to R.C. Regiment, 1843.
William Gardiner	Exchanged to 8th Regiment, 1842.
R. J. O'Flaherty	Promoted, 1845.
George Ledingham	Died at Poona, 1850.
Frederick Hobson Clark	Died at sea, 1855.
Charles F. Stephenson	Died at Deesa, 1856.
Robert Browne	Exchanged to 25th Regiment, 1863.
Chas. R. Robinson	
J. H. Macfadin	Exchanged to 47th Foot, 8th Dec., 1869.

SURGEON-MAJOR.	
A. R. Hudson	Transferred to Staff 28th March, 1879.

ASSISTANT-SURGEONS.	
George R. Watson	Died at Ballinrobe, 1882.
David Pitcairn	Exchanged to 15th Hussars, 1854.
James Flyter	Exchanged to 4th Dragoon Guards, 1847.
James Macbeth	Removed to Staff, 1843.
John H. Ker Innes	To Staff, 1851.
W. S. S. H. Monro	Retired, 1855.
John Hamilton Bews	To Staff (promoted), 1855.
W. N. Boyce	Died at Kurrachee, 1862.
Edward Touch	Promoted to Staff, 1857.
H. C. Miles	Promoted.
William Sharp	Half-pay.

Assistant-Surgeons.	Remarks.
Thomas Mould	Transferred to Royal Artillery, 1862.
C. S. Wills	
J. Bourke	Exchanged to 2nd 15th Regiment, 10th February, 1869.
E. Coffey	Transferred to Staff 6th March, 1870.
W. Geoghan	
T. G. Adye Curran	Transferred, 1874.

THE END

www.ingramcontent.com/pod-product-compliance
Lightning Source LLC
Chambersburg PA
CBHW032131090426

4274 3CB00007B/558